Income Investing
EXPLAINED
Your Questions Answered

Henry Mah, CMA

Disclaimer

The information and opinions in this book must not be considered investment advice. The information is intended to be for informational purposes only. I am not an investment advisor and I am not recommending any security or investment product.

Opinions offered here can never be a substitution for independent analysis and due diligence. The book may contain some forward-looking statements and opinions on subject matter that is familiar and already well-covered. Your guess as to the future value of any security is as good as mine, or that of a broker. Forecasting is an unreliable enterprise.

There are always risks involved with investing, and investors must expect occasional losses on the risks they take. It is certain there will be periods of time when all investing strategies, including Income growth investing, will underperform the market. It is always best to have measured expectations when approaching investing in any form.

Copyright © 2020 Henry Mah, CMA

All rights reserved.

ISBN: 9781777241001

I dedicate this book to all those who contacted me with questions, requests, provided feedback, and for their kind words letting me know that the Income Growth Investment Strategy has helped them.

Special thanks to my daughter Theresa for reading through my earlier drafts, correcting my grammatical errors and reminding me, on many occasions, that what I wrote just didn't make sense.

Foreword

Henry's most recent and third book, *Income Investing Explained*, comes out as the next great financial crisis may or may not be unfolding, although it may not seem like we ever really got over the last one. Indeed, in response to COVID-19, today's governments and central banks are employing the same recipe of interest rate cuts, stimulus spending, and quantitative easing as they did after 2008, albeit with exponentially greater debt under their belts and far less rate to cut. Past official actions set the table for the longest-ever bull market in the 2010s, much as present-day decisions will define the financial landscape of the 2020s.

At the moment (as of mid-August 2020), ongoing quantitative easing has staved off despair and continues to prop up the market; many tech darlings have, in fact, pushed past pre-pandemic levels to new highs, and the S&P 500 as an index repeatedly flirted with its previous all-time high before briefly setting a new record during the Aug. 18 trading day. The recovery of the S&P/TSX composite has been somewhat less robust, not yet setting new records, but is nonetheless remarkable considering its outlook last March.

But all this could change tomorrow. Whether world economies will bounce back quickly and substantially enough to make up for lost activity due to COVID is anyone's guess. In particular, I (and surely many other investors) wonder how markets will fare as officials move past the "emergency" phase of their pandemic plans and take a lighter hand on economic intervention. For example, we can safely assume that the end of CERB payments and other individual and corporate benefits to those who lost work or business in the last few months will weigh on share prices; there will simply be less money to go around, on everyone's part.

Factors such as the 2020 U.S. presidential campaign, federal Finance Minister Bill Morneau's abrupt resignation, and of course, the lack of a COVID vaccine or anything like a known endpoint for the pandemic, add to uncertainty and invite further volatility. That said, not all signs portend doom and gloom. The market managed to pleasantly surprise itself by overestimating the scale of losses earlier this year and could well do so again. Prior to COVID, investors had already proven themselves fairly adept at quickly forgetting about the crisis of the day (the Shanghai Stock Exchange crash, Brexit, the China-U.S. trade dispute, etc., etc.) and accentuating the positive.

The good news is that Henry's income-investing system does not depend on fickle and specific current investor confidence, in too-short supply one day and irrational overabundance the next; instead, his approach relies on a generalized, long-term belief in the economy and market. Index-based mutual funds and ETFs trade on much the same principle: even if things are or were bad, they will always get better eventually. However, by calling on investors to make more active decisions and choose their favourite dividend-payers within that overarching market context, Henry's system offers them the added bonus of insulating themselves from market setbacks, a capacity that also improves over time.

In my experience, investors tend to buy into a specific company, sector, or theme the first time they jump into the market. *Income Investing Explained* outlines a more deliberate way to invest. Whether or not his is the right approach for you, seeking greater knowledge is always a smart investment.

Robin Poon
Editor, Investor's Digest of Canada
www.adviceforinvestors.com

Introduction

This book is a result of the many emails and questions I've received since publishing my first two books *Your Ever Growing Income* and *Your TFSA Compounder*. These books discussed the Income Growth Investment Strategy that I have been researching and following, since discovering Tom Connolly and dividend growth in 2005.

I'm extremely grateful to all those who have taken the time to contact me and let me know that my books have helped them with their investment decisions. I've heard from people who are just beginning their investment journey, from experienced investors, from people who felt I added to their knowledge and even from those who have been following the Income growth strategy for years and found my process an aid to their own personal investment methods.

After writing the first two books, I received many appreciative comments that the evaluation process was simple, easy to follow and to implement. I also started a blog so that I could continue to share and discuss investment news, concentrating mostly on Income investment. Initially, I thought I could address these questions over time with my blog. But because there were so many different questions coming from people that were not associated with my online discussions, I thought many wouldn't find the answers they were seeking. Some of the questions were basic, others more advanced, like:

- How do I open an investment broker account and which broker is the best?
- How do I decide which stocks to buy and when?
- Do changing markets affect the decision-making process?
- How can I determine when a stock is under or over-valued?
- What's a good time to consider buying an expensive stock?
- How many stocks should I hold?
- Which sectors are the best to buy and invest in?
- And many others!

I will try to address all the questions and concerns I received, being as specific as I can, but I always like to stress that the recommendations, comments and suggestions will still only be my opinion, and should not be considered financial advice. You should look at this book as an addition to the Income Growth Investment Strategy that I presented in my first two books. It is further clarification of the process, and will hopefully help you in making sound investment decisions, especially during times of changing market conditions.

Any stock mentioned or used as an example to support what is being discussed, should not be taken as a stock to buy. I always want you to make your buy-decisions based upon your own evaluation and buy-criteria.

I will not be recounting in detail the Income growth evaluation process that is explained in my earlier books. For those of you not familiar with those books, I outlined a process that presented a method of how to screen stocks, where to find the data to input into Excel worksheets and how to develop, what I refer to as, your "List of Stocks to Consider". This is a list of specific stocks that you compile after careful analysis and evaluation, and that you will refer to when deciding which stocks to add to your portfolio. This book, instead, will concentrate on explaining the investment decisions you need to consider and how those decisions might change, given changes in market conditions. In other words, the decisions you make and the questions you need to ask could change depending upon current market conditions, whether the market is going up or down. And if there is a crisis, as with the current Covid-19 global health emergency, the markets often become completely unpredictable and volatile.

In most cases, there is never one answer which suits all situations, but hopefully the explanations within this book will make investing easier for the beginner, and provide some clarification to the more experienced investor. Some may think that many of the suggestions I present are all they might need to make their investment decisions, but investing is a learning process. As you become more experienced and familiar with Income growth investing, you may wish to expand or modify the strategy and add some of your own thoughts, which is what Iwould expect. I often say, don't just accept what others preach, and I include myself in that group. No one has all the answers and no one is right all the time. It is best to be as prepared and informed as you can, and I hope my book will add to your knowledge and confidence when it comes to your individual investment decisions.

Chapter 1

Opening an Investment broker account

Most likely you will already have an investment brokerage account, but I have been asked which is the best brokerage firm to use when following the Income Growth Investment Strategy.

Opening a "self-directed" investment broker account today is fairly straight-forward. In Canada, most of the major banks have investment accounts, and there are several others, such as Questrade and ShareOwners Investment Inc. to choose from.

Each will have slightly different trading commissions as well as requirements for minimum amounts held in the account:

Ranks	Broker	Basic stock-trading commission	Minimum non-registered account size for no annual/inactivity fees #	Mobile app/mobile responsive website
1	Questrade*	$4.95 min. to $9.95 max., at 1¢ per share	$5,000 or one trade *	Yes
2	Qtrade Investor	$8.75	$25,000 or eight commissioned trades	Yes
3	TD Direct Investing	$9.99	$15,000	Yes
4	Interactive Brokers	$1 min. or $0.01 per share	US$10 monthly commission or US$100,000	Yes
5	BMO InvestorLine	$9.95	$15,000	Yes

If you search the internet for the best online brokers, you will see comparisons such as:

Brand	Best For:
1. Questrade	Best for low fees
1. Qtrade	Best for customer service
1. Scotia iTrade	Best for larger deposits
1. TD Direct Investing	Best for passive investing approach
1. BMO InvestorLine Self-Directed	Best for user-friendly trading interface
1. Virtual Brokers	Best for new research
1. Wealthsimple Trade	Best for new investors
1. ShareOwners Investment Inc.	Best for dividend reinvestment

The choice of a broker can be as simple as just "sticking" with the bank where you have your chequing and savings accounts. Obviously, this will make transferring funds back and forth easier. Or you may choose to go with the broker offering the lowest trading fees, while some may wish to select a company which offers full-dividend reinvestment.

In my book, *Your TFSA Compounder*, I recommended Canadian-based ShareOwners Investment Inc. because they are the only investment broker where the dividends you receive will buy fractions of shares. With all other brokers you can only purchase a full share. If the dividend received is not large enough to buy a full share, the funds (or remaining funds after buying a full share) will be left in the account and will just sit as cash or they can be added to future purchases.

Personally, I've found that being able to buy fractions of shares, with accumulated dividends, can increase your holdings by as much as 5% to 7% over the long-term.

To better illustrate my point, here is a comparison of reinvested dividends with Synthetic (full shares) or Full Dividend Reinvestment (fractions):

	Dividend Reinvested Full Shares			Dividend Reinvested Fractional Shs		
Date	Price	Shares	Div Rec'd	Price	Shares	Div Rec'd
Aug 24\15	75.6923	3.0000	253.50	75.6923	3.3491	253.50
Nov 24\15	75.9207	3.0000	255.75	75.9207	3.3721	256.01
Feb 24\16	70.4955	3.0000	264.88	70.4955	3.7653	265.44
May 26\16	77.4355	3.0000	267.19	77.4355	3.4653	268.33
Aug 26\16	80.7956	3.0000	276.50	80.7956	3.4413	278.04
Nov 24\16	88.5534	3.0000	278.87	88.5534	3.1705	280.76
Feb 24\17	99.8366	2.0000	288.36	99.8366	2.9091	290.44
May 24\17	92.6661	3.0000	289.98	92.6661	3.1596	292.79
Aug 24\17	92.2100	3.0000	299.63	92.2100	3.2821	302.65
Nov 24\17	101.2248	3.0000	302.12	101.2248	3.0167	305.37
Feb 24\18	102.4383	3.0000	319.29	102.4383	3.1503	322.71
May 24\18	101.5316	3.0000	321.90	101.5316	3.2054	325.45
Aug 24\18	103.2386	3.0000	339.43	103.2386	3.3256	343.33
Nov 24\18	96.4340	3.0000	342.16	96.4340	3.5917	346.36
Feb 24\19	102.3171	3.0000	356.26	102.3171	3.5297	361.15
May 24\19	104.9930	3.0000	359.08	104.9930	3.4714	364.47
Aug 24\19	99.6542	3.0000	377.30	99.6542	3.8471	383.38
Nov 24\19	109.0611	3.0000	380.24	109.0611	3.5499	387.15
		53.00	$5,572.44		60.60	$5,627.34

The additional 7.6 shares (60.60-53.00) purchased through dividend reinvestment represent a 2.0% increase in the original number of shares over 4 ½ years, and the percentage will continue to grow over the years. In addition to this particularly important advantage, I like the idea of having every penny invested working as quickly as possible to grow my income. With ShareOwners you will be able to buy shares at a faster pace and enhance compounding. I'll expand on this vital concept later in the book.

As with most decisions there are trade-offs. You will find that the trading costs of ShareOwners are a bit higher, you cannot buy stocks using "Limit Orders" (stating the price you wish to buy at), not every stock qualifies for full-dividend reinvestment and their account fees will be higher than most other brokers. You must weigh these trade-offs with every broker you consider, then you will have to decide what your priorities are for your portfolio and make your choice accordingly.

After you choose your preferred broker, you will need to complete their application form, selecting the account you wish to open from these three main types:

- TFSA account
- RRSP account
- Non-registered account

I strongly advise that you do not open a "Margin" account. A margin account is one where you'll be able to borrow money to buy shares. Depending upon your financial status and credit rating, you might be able to borrow up to 50% of the cost to purchase stocks. However, I do not recommend starting this habit, I don't think it is a good idea to start your investment journey by going into debt.

Chapter 2

Income Investing

There are many ways to invest in stocks and each has their advantages and disadvantages. Some people will find one strategy more attractive than others; you may even wish to combine several strategies. The choice is yours. However, having the ability to evaluate any strategy is the key, and often investors have no idea how to decide which method to follow or how to select and implement their strategy of choice.

What makes Income investing unique from all other strategies, is that it is a "feel-good, all-the-time" strategy. Think about it. All other investors feel really good when stock prices are rising, but less so when prices drop. They feel terrible when there is a market crash, unless they are able to sell before prices drop. Should the market tumble, and they still hold stocks, they worry about how long the market will stay down or how long it will take for the market and the value of their stocks to recover.

Income investors look at the stocks they own differently. Sure, they want to buy at the lowest price possible, but it's not the price that attracts them, it's the **income** the stocks will provide. Every time an Income investor buys stocks, they know they will be earning more income from their investments regardless of market conditions:

- When the markets are rising, the company stocks they own are more likely to raise their dividend, which means more income.

- When stock prices tumble, or there is a market correction, the lower prices allow one to buy more shares with less money, thereby increasing their income.

- Whether markets are up or down, reinvesting their dividends will generate more income.

- When a company raises their dividend, their income from all of the shares they own, of that company, will pay them more income.

So, as you can see, by following the Income Growth Investment Strategy, the income from your investments will grow regardless of what the market is doing. Imagine, not having to watch the market results each day, worry about economic news which might affect stock prices and know that even if the value of your holdings drops, your income should continue to grow.

All these reasons are why I have chosen Income investing. Through personal experience and research, I have come to know that the Income Growth Investment Strategy is the safest and only strategy that has given me and my wife the opportunity to live off our income. Many people have shared this approach to investing for years, and I have taken much from their experiences and findings. But I needed to understand it even more deeply and thoroughly so that I could make even better-informed decisions. Everyone has access to the same information, but I found that much of the available information and evaluation processes were overly-complicated and difficult to apply. I wanted to develop a process that takes all this information, simplifies it, and would allow me to use it in a sensible straightforward way. What I found was that some of the best things about this particular strategy are:

- The evaluation and selection process for screening and selecting stocks is easy and does not require extensive analysis.

- The data you need to perform your analysis is readily available and needs only be entered into an Excel worksheet to provide the information needed.

- Once you've made your selection of stocks to consider, there is no need to re-do or re-evaluate the stocks on your list for many years.

- You don't need to find a large number of stocks for your list, but instead a smaller number of the best stocks that you like.

- You only need to look at stocks that have a long history of paying and growing the income they pay to shareholders.

- Once you have made your selection, you don't have to look for new stock or better stocks.

- When you wish to buy shares, you just look at the stocks on your pre-vetted list which offer a reasonable yield.

- Once you've made a purchase, ignore the future price movement of the stocks you own.

- The monitoring of the stocks you own is as simple as recording the dividends paid, dividend increases and the growth of your total income.

- By sticking with the best Income stock, you will reduce the risk of losing money, and increase your potential income.

Which stocks? The 1% Solution

Income investing is about buying stocks which will pay you income for owning their company shares, and grow the income they pay over time. It really is as simple as that. But I have come to realize that many of the stocks which might fall under that description are not necessarily ones which you should contemplate buying. I believe every stock has a "story", and investors need to know that history before considering adding it to their portfolio. By taking the time to screen and eliminate as many stocks as you can, you'll ensure a steady stream of income, greatly increase your potential income and reduce much of the risk associated with investing.

After my own deliberations and analysis, I have come to the conclusion that only about 1% of the stocks listed on the Canadian and US Indexes should be considered Quality Dividend Growth stocks. Imagine, ignoring 99% of the stocks listed on the TSX Composite and S&P 500 indexes when you are doing your evaluation and making your investment choices. Does that make any sense? Does it even seem feasible? Probably 99% of investors, advisors and financial writers would say, Never. The majority of investors look for growth stocks, which are moving targets.Meaning they are rarely the same companies each year, and you won't know which have been the best performersuntil after the fact. Not so with dividend growth stocks,these can easily be identified, and their performance confirmed each quarter.

I'm suggesting that there are about 40 Canadian and 50 US companies that possess the qualities of a **good** dividend growth stock. In fact, most people are aware of many of them, they consider them well-established, large and stable companies. Many will be household names and companies which provide products and services we use or need regularly. One could probably name 10-15 without doing any research. Not all might exactly fit my criteria for quality dividend growth stocks, but most will be ones which should be taken into consideration.

That's what Income investing is all about; finding a select few, just the 1% or less, of the companies that pay and increase the payments they make to shareholders. They won't be the super-growth companies or the ones which are highly under-valued, but they will be companies which generate regular and steady earnings.

By following the Income Growth Investment Strategy and investing in just those few companies, that 1%, you'll obtain financial freedom slowly and steadily. Bet on it.

I have always been reluctant to just "hand out" a list of my current holdings or preferred stocks. For one thing, my choices are personal, based on a set of individual priorities and criteria. I would be remiss to suggest that my criteria will match every other investor's needs, especially when they implement the process or select stocks to purchase at their own time and pace. And no matter which stocks are on my list, they were chosen at a specific point in time, and may not even be choices I'd make if I performed an evaluation today. **So, instead of asking "which", ask "how"**. Every investor needs to learn to do their own evaluation, make their selection and decide the best choices for them, at that time. And that is why I created an evaluation process that I believe anyone can use to create a list of stocks that should meet their particular needs. And it can be applied and used at any time, during any market conditions.

For this book, I've chosen 45 Canadian dividend growth stocks and 35 US dividend growth stocks for your consideration. And remember that by calling them "dividend growth stocks", I mean those Canadian and US stocks which have a long history of paying and growing their dividend at a reasonably high rate. I think you will find that most are familiar company names. As of this writing all of the Canadian stocks have raised their dividend over the past 10 years and the US companies have raised theirs for at least 25 years. (See Appendix A for the 45 Canadian stocks and Appendix B for the US stocks.)

I've selected these stocks not because they are the best of the best, but because they are generally recognized as quality dividend growth stocks. The stocks on these two lists are ones that have increased their dividend consecutively for many years, and hopefully, will continue to be good stocks for the foreseeable future.

Wait a minute, did I just suggest something I've tried to preach against? Don't listen to, or accept recommendations from others, without doing your own research and screening, and that includes me!

Don't just assume that these 45 Canadian and 35 US stocks listed as being "quality dividend growth stocks" should automatically be added to

your "List of Stocks to Consider". Instead, take the time to apply the analysis, which I've explained in great detail in my earlier books, to narrow your selection. My process makes the important assumption that it is reasonable to expect your choices to meet some basic minimum requirements. It is intended to help you to quickly screen stocks. I also suggest adding some of your own criteria to decide which stocks you feel most comfortable with, and which you might consider buying. I think it a wise decision to make stock purchasing a more personal experience. This is why I choose not to use a financial advisor or lose my way in an ocean of advice and opinions.

This an important lesson I would like you to learn: **that what others consider the "best", or stocks they might recommend, may not actually be the best stocks for you.** This is why I mentioned earlier that there is no "best of the best" without further analysis, especially when the creation of any list of potential stocks needs to involve your own research. As an investor, do you know how people (and I mean "financial advisors") evaluate stocks, when the evaluation is done and if the expected results may be valid? Can you even be sure their goals will meet your particular goals?Don't get excited by others recommendations and hot tips, make your own selections and use your own judgement.

I also intentionally "left in" a few stocks (in the lists of the 45 Canadian and 35 US stocks) that I had cut from my own list, after applying my stock screening process, to demonstrate that sometimes even the "best" long-time dividend growth stocks might not be the best stocks to consider.

For the beginning investor, I recommend that you review the stocks with the objective of creating a small, but select "List of Stocks to Consider". Don't feel you need to have dozens of stocks on your list right off the bat. When it comes to deciding which stocks to eventually buy, your decision will be easier if the list is smaller, rather than larger. Also, don't start your stock selection with a specific stock or sector in mind. My system of evaluation helps you screen and decide on just a few of the best stocks, regardless which sector you find them. Once you've completed the first pass, look at the data carefully, to see if you like your choices. You are trying to refine the list to a more manageable number. You can always add additional stocks. Don't worry if this seems daunting, I will be discussing this process later in the book.

Learn to do it yourself, without ETFs

A lot of people assume stock market investing is overly complicated and risky, especially when it comes to picking individual stocks. I feel strongly that the average investor has been made to feel inadequate to make their own decisions. As well, because people don't want to learn more about the market and its behaviour, they'd rather just let someone else do the work.

I keep hearing about Index ETF funds, how popular they are and how highly recommended they have become. I agree that they are easy to invest in and they will grow in accordance with the market, but I think there are some very specific reasons why ETFs have become so ubiquitous. Most investors have been led to believe that getting market returns is sufficient, something ETFs are very good at providing. Index ETFs will give investors close to market returns, and even some distribution income. But market returns are not always positive and ETF distributions have a tendency to fluctuate with the market. As I write this book, the world is experiencing the Covid-19 global health crisis and the long-term effects are still unknown. Many businesses were forced to close, lay off staff, defer payments and millions have suffered from a major loss of income.

How quickly businesses will recover, or when things will get back to normal, is a big unknown. The longer the crisis continues, the deeper the effects it will have on businesses and the market. If the market suffers, and it has, so will the ETFs, because Index funds hold all the stocks making up the market or Index. There will be many companies that may have to cut their dividend and that will be reflected in lower ETF distributions.

But the question I ask is, that so many do not, are Index ETFs as simple to invest in as most believe? Certainly, you can use recommendations from others on which funds to buy, but there are so many ETFs to choose from, that include so many different stocks, how will you know which one is best? Is there an evaluation process for ETFs or do they all perform the same, as in, do they all give you the same market returns? Is it just that easy?

I ask you to consider the following:

- *There are 45 Vanguard ETFs Trading on the Toronto Stock Exchange.*

INCOME INVESTING EXPLAINED

- *There are 134 iShares ETFs trading on the Toronto Stock Exchange.*

- *There are 115 BMO ETFs Trading on the Toronto Stock Exchange.*

- *Some of the other Canadian ETF providers include AGF, Claymore, Hamilton, Horizon, First Assets, Purpose, Wisdom, Invesco, First Trust, plus 10 or more others, all offering a large number of ETFs.*

- *There are more than 2,200 exchange traded products (ETFs) trading in the U.S.*

- *There are 5,024 ETFs trading globally.*

Apparently, there are almost 500 ETFs traded in Canada, and the number of stocks within each ETF can vary from less than a hundred to over twelve thousand. Trying to decide which provider and which ETF to choose can be quite the challenge.

I think it is just as fair to ask, can selecting a **small** number of quality dividend growth stocks be any more difficult or daunting? The fact that so many investors do not make their own choices would indicate the answer is yes. But I do not think so.

Remember, Income investing is not about selecting stocks at random, just from the **1%** of the quality dividend growth stocks you've screened from the Canadian TSX Composite index and the US, S & P 500. And, even then, I recommend to narrow down your choices even further.

If the benefit of investing in ETFs, which holds all the stocks of an index, is their safe and predictable market returns, then having a small select portfolio of hand-picked quality dividend growth stocks from the same Index, should be an even more desired investment for income.

By selecting from a few of the best dividend growth stocks, you will maintain a much greater sense of control and security. I firmly believe you are better off with a small but well-appraised stock portfolio than an Index full of unknowns. By learning the basics of Income growth investing you will discover it is no more difficult to manage a portfolio of quality individual stocks, than it is to assume safety by investing in ETFs.

Income investing is not about obtaining average market returns from a huge index, but earning a predictable income and better returns from a small portfolio of carefully chosen stocks. I think it is also important to note that ETFs have attracted many investors through a lower fee structure, but there are still fees and as your investment and ETFs grow in value, the larger the fee becomes. With a self-directed investment portfolio, you won't pay any of these fees, so every dollar invested will go to growing your income.

Getting started is often the hardest part of any journey, but once you've completed the initial steps of Income investing, finding the road to success becomes much easier.

The Five Guiding Rules:

It is important for me to note here that I developed a Four-Rule test to evaluate stocks and described it in detail in my first two books. For those that have read my earlier books, you will be familiar with my four-rule test, as it really is the backbone of my strategy. It is essentially a "questionnaire", an analysis that you apply to any stock to help you determine if it is a quality dividend growth stock. I am providing the rules here for the new reader, and I am also now adding a **fifth rule**:

1. Has the company cut their dividend in the past 10 years: Yes or No?
2. Has the company paid a dividend, for a minimum of 10 years (25 years or more is even better)?
3. Has the company had a consistent record of raising their dividend for 10 years? (The more often the increase, the better the stock).
4. Has the dividend grown over the past 10 years by at least 75%?
5. If a stock has not increased their dividend by at least 3%, for the past three years, each year over the previous year, it should be excluded.

Rule #1 is fixed because companies that cut their dividend are either a cyclical stock or it's a sign that the company has had financial problems. We want to avoid cyclical stocks because we are seeking **reliable** income from the companies we choose. Any company which has cut their dividend will likely take many years before they are able to begin increasing the dividend again.

The other four rules are a little more flexible, there may be companies and situations where you will wish to make an exception by including them in your "List of Stocks to Consider", even though they don't meet 100% of the criteria. The fifth rule was added because I want to stress the importance of continuing to monitor a stock's "fitness". A negative answer to this statement may indicate that the company's growth has slowed, that the dividend growth might be lower than desired and that the company's earnings may be faltering.

I have always provided "exceptions" to this list of rules. I think it is important to be flexible when evaluating a company and stock. There are many factors that come into play when dealing with a large company and its performance history. Let's look at three different "exception" scenarios for your consideration:

1. **A company has paid and raised their dividend for 10 years, but the dividend growth is less than 75%.**

This is an example of an exception because there are companies, like utilities, that have raised their dividend for many years, I like to call them the "Steady Eddies". Many of them post a 5% dividend increase over 10 years which provides a 63% dividend growth, below our 75%, but I still consider them an attractive stock choice.

One must also consider that since the financial crisis of 2008 and low interest rates the dividend growth rates have slowed for many companies. This kind of fluctuation should not necessarily cancel a good long-time performing stock from your list. Regardless of the example of sub-75% dividend growth, you will have to consider all aspects of any given situation and decide if you wish to add a company with a lower dividend growth rate to your list.

1. **A company has only paid a dividend for 8 or 9 years (which is less than the 10-year minimum), but posts a better-than 75% growth.**

There are plenty of examples of a company paying a dividend for less than the ideal 10-year minimum time period, raising their dividend yearly and posting a growth rate at or above 75%. (By less than 10 years, I mean between 8 and 9 years. Anything less would be too short a time period for serious consideration). These companies might be considered new dividend growers and should be looked at seriously.

1. **A company has paid a dividend for 10 years, but not grown the dividend each year (perhaps 7 of 10 years) and has a lower than 75% dividend growth rate.**

Most Canadian banks are examples of this exception. For example, in 2008 they were discouraged from raising their dividend until their financial reserves were higher. Beyond this development, and for many years before, their growth was steady, their dividend payout and dividend increases exceptional. My experience with Canadian bank stocks is that they are generally secure long-term dividend growth investments.

There will always be exceptions to any rule, but consider each separately, for they may not be applicable to every situation. I might consider a 10-year dividend growth rate of 60% as my minimum threshold, but there may be a good stock with 58% that I'd consider buying, because I feel the stock has great future growth potential. Yet I may not want to consider any number of other stocks which only offer a 75% dividend growth rate, even if others feel they have great growth potential. Personal judgement will carry much more weight when considering exceptions than fixed numbers or recommendations by others. Look at each exception you are considering as a unique situation.

Why I added Rule #5

Having the income paid by companies grow is one of the most important aspects of investing for Income. But it's not a fixed requirement, which will be discussed later in the book. However, the five-rules are intended to assist you in developing a list of stocks to consider buying. The first four rules will narrow your selection by looking at a company history over a 10-year period, while the fifth rule provides you an indication of how the company is performing in more recent times.

When a company has had several years of good dividend growth, but then the dividend growth drops below 3%, it may be a sign that the company is having difficulty meeting its current dividend payment. If the dividend growth continues to be below 3% for the next year, it's likely the company is increasing the dividend by a minimum amount in order to maintain its continuous record of growing its dividend each year. Even worse, the company may be experiencing financial difficulty.

	2010	2011	2012	2013	2014	2015	2016	2017	2018	2019	10 Yr Gth%
Dividend	1.21	1.46	1.59	1.88	1.92	1.96	2.00	2.04	2.08	2.12	75.21%
Div Gth Yr		20.66%	8.90%	18.24%	2.13%	2.08%	2.04%	2.00%	1.96%	1.92%	

The example above shows that, at the beginning of 2014, the dividend growth of this particular company dropped below 3% and continued to drop each year thereafter. By 2015, the second year with below 3% dividend growth, I think one should be hesitant to consider adding new funds to this stock.

It should be clear that as each year passes, to 2020, 2021, etc., the 10-year dividend growth rate for this company will begin to drop, unless the company begins to raise the dividend at a much higher percentage.

Now, if you've owned the stock for many years, you may be willing to continue to hold the stock. Even with the low dividend growth, the income you receive and the yield on your investment of the stock may make it worth continuing to hold, but I would not recommend buying more of this company's shares until the year-to-year dividend growth percentage increases. Instead, you may wish to mark this stock as one you might consider selling, at the right price, and look for another stock which is offering a higher dividend growth rate.

A long history of paying and growing the dividend is how we determine which stocks to consider, but looking into the future is not as clear. That's why you need to seek markers which might indicate that the past history will continue or at least will help you in determining which companies are more likely to be able to maintain growing their dividend.

How many stocks on your list?

The number of stocks you decide to add to your "List of Stocks to Consider" is a personal choice. But as this book is intended to guide you in setting up an Income growth portfolio, I strongly suggest you begin with a smaller number of stocks, rather than the longest list possible.

As suggested earlier, I believe there are around 40 Canadian and 50 US companies which might meet my initial guidelines. Those are your starting stocks to consider, not the ones which should be on your final list of stocks. The main purpose of applying the five-rule test is to screen out stocks which may be less desirable, or of lower quality, based on their performance over the previous 10-year period. Once you have completed your evaluation, I suggest no more than 20 to 30 in each of your Canadian and US companies "List of Stocks to Consider". These lists will include all the Canadian and US stocks you will monitor and choose from when you are ready to buy. This should enable you to find three or four stocks in each of the major sectors and provide sufficient diversification.

Remember, you do not have to own all of the stocks on your list, but you'll review and select from these stocks, depending upon:

- the yield they offer,
- the sector they are in, and
- the account you are buying the stocks for.

No, you don't need to hold stocks in every sector

Most advisors recommend you diversify your holdings in order to take advantage of the fact that different sectors react differently to various market conditions. The logic being that if one sector is not doing well, another will, offsetting any potential loss. Maybe that's fine for those worried about capital growth. For Income investors, we are more selective because not all sectors contain stocks which will provide reliable dividend growth. You want to avoid cyclical stocks, which will include most, if not all, energy, mining, transportation, housing, technology, and some durable and soft goods stocks. Any product or service which would be affected by changes in the overall economy should be avoided as well. I exclude most pipeline companies as they are more like a utility. Some cyclical sectors may have a good dividend growth stock, but I'd be very selective before adding one.

If you narrow your choice to 20 to 30 quality dividend growth stocks, it's likely you will be able to find ones which provide a reasonable yield and in a sector of your choice when you are ready to purchase. Remember that various stocks and market sectors will react differently to current events, as will stock prices in those sectors. Even though price and market value is not our main objective, you will want to have sufficient stocks on your list to allow for these market changes and allow you to find a stock that offers a reasonable yield, when you have money to invest. Don't get hung up on believing you need to own stocks in every sector or market to be diversified. You can have adequate diversification by holding two or three dividend growth stocks in as few as five to seven sectors.

Stop looking for new stocks

I've emphasized in each of my books that once you've compiled your "List of Stocks to Consider", there will be little need to redo the list or constantly be on the lookout for new stocks. You are evaluating stocks by looking at their past 10-year performance and determining how you feel about them at the time. You may even ask yourself if you believe their future prospects look bright enough in the next few years. Once satisfied, close your eyes and ears to all other stocks.

Don't get caught up with the hype or suggestions of industry advisors or headlines in the news and add just for the sake of having more to choose from. I've received several responses from readers telling me of instances where they bought a stock with less than 10 years of dividend payments or growth, but it had high dividend growth over 5 or 6 years. Then once the Covid-19 crisis hit they were surprised by a dividend cut.

If you've taken the time to evaluate the majority of Canadian dividend growth stocks, I recommend that you decide upon 20 to 30, for your list, and not many more. Trust me, there won't really be that many good candidates left to consider. Also, don't feel you need to immediately remove a company from your list if they do not increase their dividend or if they are affected by financial or economic issues and cut their dividend. You just don't have to buy that particular stock, but you can continue to monitor it, should it become more attractive later. At some later date, after further analysis, you may wish to get rid of it completely, or any others, and look for a new or replacement stock for your list.

Should you become aware of a new stock, take the time to evaluate it and if you believe it worthy, then add it to your list. But adding more stocks should be the exception, not the rule.

> *If you can identify twenty successful companies that can maintain a 5% to 8% dividend growth rate, each and every year, and your portfolio consists of just those stocks, I am confident you will retire with more income than you can spend.*

Don't instantly get hooked on companies that grow their dividend by 10% or more each year. There are only a few dividend paying stocks which will provide an annual dividend growth of 10% or more, each year, for an extended number of years. Companies which are able to grow their dividend over 10% each year usually provide a low initial yield. They will be the growth stocks whose price grows at a fairly high rate. Remember if the price rises the dividend yield falls. You may wish to own a few of those low-yield, high-growth stocks, but the majority of your holdings should provide an average initial yield and average dividend growth.

By "average" I am referring to those companies with an initial yield of between 3% to 5%, a 10-year growth rate of 75% or higher, a dividend increase of 5% or more each and every year over the long-term, and that can be purchased with a yield close to or above their 10-year average.

Another interesting aspect of a quality dividend growth stock is that they don't change much over time. They are not the companies where you'll see the stock price double each year or be on any financial guru's "Top Stocks" list. The best of these types of stocks will provide slow and steady growth in both the dividend and price. And that is why Income investing works. But the process requires patience and discipline to let these "Steady Eddies" do what they do best.

In essence, by concentrating on just 1% of the stocks within the market, we are giving up the opportunity of holding some high growth stocks for the more secure quality stocks which provide us with a steady stream of income.

With the Income Growth Investment Strategy, you will be able to ignore changes in the stock market, feel confident in your choice of stocks and not be as concerned about when to purchase them.

Yes, bad things can and will happen, and some may well experience a reversal of fortunes, but as an Income investor, you will likely see the signs and have a chance to take action. I'll discuss some of these situations and what to do later in the book.

What is stock market risk?

We have all heard about Investing Risk. Many times, they are referring to Risk Tolerance.

> *Market risk* is the possibility of an investor experiencing losses due to factors that affect the overall performance of the financial markets in which he or she is involved. Market risk is the risk of losses on financial investments **caused by adverse price movements.**
>
> *Risk tolerance* (the degree of uncertainty you are willing to take on to achieve potentially greater rewards) is determined by a combination of factors, including your investment goals and experience, how much time you have to invest, your other financial resources and your *"fear factor."*

So, risk is the real possibility of losing money because the price of the stocks you own may go down. But one only loses money from stocks if they sell their shares when the price has gone down. I don't know how many companies listed on the Canadian or US stock markets that actually go out of business, or where the value of their stock becomes zero, but I would hesitate to suggest that even 10% do. The majority which do fail are likely new companies, and those in a cyclical sector, such as mining, technology and commodities.

For the vast majority of stocks listed on various Indexes, especially the 1% well-established companies, the chance of their stock prices dropping to zero will be extremely small. They are not immune to price fluctuation, but over the long-term their stock price will recover as the market recovers. Some might merge or be taken over by another company, so your existing holdings would be replaced with the new stock. The most recent Canadian example was the merger of Potash and Agrium, forming Nutrien in early 2018.

Stocks for various investment accounts

But first let's talk about debt

Before discussing which accounts to invest your funds in, it might be prudent to mention **debt**. If you have debt, even if you consider your debts manageable, you may be better off paying down your debt before investing. Take the time to work through the numbers and consider the risks involved with

investing in the stock market while you are still in debt. You may come to the conclusion that you might be better off paying off debt, including reducing your home mortgage, before you start to save for retirement in earnest.

I will stress that one should **NEVER** carry high-interest debt, such as credit cards or even student loans (Canada Student Loans' 2019 current variable rate is 6.45%, the fixed rate is 8.95%). If you can't or don't pay off your credit card balance or any other high interest loans monthly, don't even think of investing or saving yet! Pay off those high interest debts immediately. I'm not suggesting one cannot borrow money to purchase large items, but make sure you can afford to meet that debt obligation and, hopefully, pay it back sooner rather than later.

DRIP accounts:

Dividend Reinvestment Plans (DRIP) allow you to automatically reinvest the cash dividends you earn from your equity investments to buy fractions of shares. Unfortunately, not all companies which offer dividend reinvestment plans also allow you to buy additional shares without paying commissions (Share Purchase Plans SPPs). Most notably, Royal and TD bank are two examples of this. It's this combination of both a DRIP and SPP, which makes owning these shares a valuable investment choice. DRIP accounts are also non-registered accounts which will result in the dividends being taxed in the year received.

If you are not familiar with this type of account, I suggest you visit the Drip Primer website:

http://www.dripprimer.ca/aboutdrips

I especially recommend a DRIP account for anyone wishing to open an investment account for a child (other than an RESP), or if one has small amounts to invest and can only add funds periodically. The DRIP's main advantages are:

1. Once established, you can invest small amounts, even as low as $25.00, and pay no commission.
2. Every cent invested will generate dividends and those dividends will purchase fractions of shares at no cost.
3. Additional funds can be added to buy shares, including fractions of shares, at no cost.
4. Compounding is accelerated because there are no transaction fees, and every cent added to the investment account buys fractions of shares.

If an account is opened for a child, the account will need to be a joint account with an adult. In these cases, the dividends will be claimed, as taxable income, by the adult until the child turns 18. At that age, the account can be transferred to the child's name, and they would claim the dividends as income from that point onwards. **Anyone with low taxable income ($40,000 or less)** will find the tax on the dividends to be minimal or they may pay no tax at all.

There are only a few good quality dividend growth stocks which you might wish to include in a DRIP account. These may include the following:

Three Banks:

BMO – paid a dividend since 1820's
BNS – paid a dividend since 1932
CIBC – paid a dividend since 1868

Two Utility Companies:

Emera– Utility Company
Fortis – Long history of raising its dividend

Two Communication Companies:

BCE – largest Communication Company in Canada
Telus – A company with one with the best dividend history

One Pipeline:

TC Energy – Held dividend through financial crisis

One Insurance Company:

Sun Life Financial

Remember, that when considering DRIP companies, we want to ensure that you will be able to buy additional shares and be able to invest small amounts, without having to pay commissions. Because there are just not that many companies which qualify and can even decrease when you apply the five-rule test, you might consider loosening those guidelines for DRIP accounts, as long as the company has an even longer dividend history than 10 years. Rule #1 would still stay as is, fixed.

Should a DRIP be setup for a child, at age 18 when they take over the plan and it is transferred into their own name, they can continue adding funds to buy shares, reinvest the dividends, purchase fractions of shares, all without fees.

They will be required to claim the dividends as taxable income, but it is unlikely they will be taxed. Once the account owner begins earning sufficient income to be taxable, the shares can be transferred to a TFSA account, allowing the funds to continue to grow and compound tax-free.

TFSA accounts:

The TFSA is an ideal account to invest in for Income growth. My second book, *Your TFSA Compounder*, explains in detail the income growth potential of a TFSA, especially when you maximize your contributions. The major advantage of investing the maximum amount, as quickly as possible, is that all the growth from your investments, as well as the compound growth, will be tax-free upon withdrawal of the funds.

I will always recommend that regardless of your age, you try to reach your maximum TFSA contribution limit as soon as you can and continue to invest the maximum amount allowed each year.

Within your TFSA, avoid fixed assets (GICs, Bonds and Preferred shares), high-yielding stocks, cyclical stocks, ETFs, Income trusts, US stocks, and even REITs. Stick with quality Canadian dividend growth stocks which offer an initial dividend yield of 3.5% to 5% and have at least a 10-year history of growing their dividend by at least 5% to 8% a year. You could add a low-yield, high-growth stock (like CNR or MRU), but keep the majority of your TFSA investments in average dividend growth stocks. We want to insure your TFSA provides consistent, and steady growth, not quick and unsustainable growth.

Don't get greedy and look at stocks which pay a higher initial yield, like 6% or above, and a dividend growth rate below 5% per year. Also, don't feel you need to hold a lot of stocks in your TFSA. Again, it's a personal choice, but I'd suggest 5 to 7 stocks in 3 or 4 different sectors. That should give you sufficient diversification and allow you to find stocks offering a reasonable yield when you are looking to buy. If you have a spousal TFSA, you could select different stocks for that account, providing greater diversification, and twice the tax-free savings.

If possible, contribute as much as you can at the beginning of each year. TFSA annual contribution begins January 1st of each year. By contributing funds (especially the maximum) as early in the year as possible, you'll put your money to work generating income as quickly as possible. Although some investors concentrate on and defer to the capital growth of their TFSA holdings, the Income investor wants to see continuous income growth, growth which should not be affected by changes in the market or the price of individual stocks. Income investors will also see capital growth as their income grows, a nice side benefit, but not the goal.

I wrote my second book, *The TFSA Compounder* specifically because I believe the TFSA and the Income Growth Investment Strategy were made for each other. I firmly believe that the TFSA, coupled with Income investing, is one of the smartest and most under-appreciated investment combinations available to Canadians. It is a steady, long-term, secure income-building strategy, with no tax penalties. What more could one ask for?

RRSP accounts:

If you have invested the maximum amount allowed to your TFSA, and to your spouse's TFSA account (when applicable), then you can begin adding funds to an RRSP. The exception to this rule will be if you have a matching company RRSP plan. It is wise to take advantage of such an investment vehicle when it is available. Never turn down free money when offered!

If contributing to an RRSP, this might be the time to add US dividend growth stocks to your portfolio. Take the time to develop a "US List of Stocks to Consider", just as you did with Canadian stocks. I suggest you begin with the 35 US Dividend Growth Stocks listed in Appendix B. There are a few things to keep in mind before buying US stocks though. These include some of the following:

- The Canadian exchange rate is currently about 30%, which means it will cost you 30% more in Canadian dollars to buy US shares.

- Personally, I think any conversion rate above $1.20, or 20%, is too high to pay for US stocks.

- US stocks have provided a higher dividend growth rate than Canadian stocks, so it makes sense to include some US stocks in your portfolio, provided you are not paying too high an amount for the exchange rate.

- The dividends will be paid in US dollars, which means you'll earn more income from the higher US dollar, as long as the exchange rate remains high.

- You can find several US multi-national companies which will take advantage of International or Emerging markets, without needing to buy foreign company stocks.

- The 15% withholding tax on the US dividends is exempt when US stocks are held in an RRSP.

Within an RRSP one might consider holding 5 to 10 US stocks and a similar number of Canadian stocks. This should allow for adequate diversification and the ability to find good quality stocks offering a reasonable yield when you have funds to invest. Remember, investing should be considered a long-term venture. Regardless of what the current market situation is, over the long-term, you'll benefit from owning some quality US dividend growth stocks in your RRSP.

Again, as an Income investor, you want to generate the maximum amount of income from your investments. By including US stocks, which have generally grown their income at a higher rate than most Canadian equities, you will have access to larger companies and some with more International exposure. But do not delude yourself that you will generate the same amount of income by owning a US ETF. (Just like owning a Canadian ETF, your income diminishes, and you would do better to concentrate on owning fewer quality dividend growth stocks.) Another benefit of the higher rate of US stocks is that you may reach a point where your required RRSP withdrawals might be covered by the income growth, not requiring any capital withdrawals. This may eliminate any concern of a market correction which could wipe out a large percentage of your investment holdings.

RESP accounts:

The Canada Revenue Agency registers the education savings plan contract as an RESP (Registered Education Savings Plan), and lifetime limits are set by the Income Tax Act on the amount that can be contributed for each beneficiary.

The funds and growth of the funds within an RESP are intended to be used for your children's education costs. The advantage of this account is that the Canadian government will match funds, to a maximum limit, until they reach the age of 18. This is another opportunity to take advantage of "free money", so to speak, which anyone with young children should take advantage of.

A safe and secure investment choice is vital for an RESP. I'm not saying you can't or shouldn't invest in stocks, but I would not recommend anything but the safest of stocks. Another consideration is the length of time before the child might need to draw down money from the account. If you expect the child will be using the money within five years, I'd suggest sticking with GICs.

However, if funds will not be needed for five years or more, than you will be better off investing in some quality, and I mean **quality**, Canadian dividend growth stocks. I talked about the "Steady Eddie" stocks in my first book. These stocks have paid and grown their dividend for a minimum of 10 years, likely even longer, and the dividend growth has averaged at least 5% each year. I suggest investing in a Canadian bank or utility stock, if you go this route. 2 to 3 stocks should be all you might need for an RESP account.

Don't worry about buying stock at the lowest price, but make sure to contribute the maximum allowed to get the maximum government contribution, as soon as you have the funds to invest. In an ideal situation, you will open an RESP soon after your child(ren) are born. There are potentially 18 years of income accumulation at your disposal, and with a portfolio of solid dividend growth stocks, your children will have a healthy amount of money available to them. A debt-free post-secondary education is a wonderful gift to give your children, and you get peace of mind as well!

Non-registered accounts:

Non-registered accounts are where the dividends received will be taxed in the year they are received. Normally, you will invest in these accounts once you've maximized your TFSA, RESP (if applicable) and RRSP accounts.

There have been arguments that one might be better off investing in a non-registered account rather than investing in an RRSP. The reasoning behind this argument is that the tax on future RRSP capital withdrawals may work out to be higher than the tax on dividends received, and tax on capital gains when stocks are sold from a non-registered account at a later date. I'm not espousing one account over the other, in fact I think you will do better investing funds in an RRSP. It's just something to take into consideration.

So, what type of stocks should you consider for a non-registered account? I still believe one should stick with dividend growth stocks, no matter what the account. Below I have provided an excerpt from my first book that emphasizes the advantage of investing in dividend growth stocks:

> *Here's the most important takeaway from my entire investing philosophy, **if you invest in quality dividend growth stocks to generate an income, the companies contribute by paying you a dividend. You reinvest the dividends to buy more shares and increase your income. When the companies raise the dividend, you will further grow your income on the shares you own. You should continue to add funds and the process accelerates. In other words, the companies are helping you to grow your income by adding to what you contribute, so you don't need to save as much to reach your income goal!***

Some have suggested buying stocks which do not pay any dividend within your non-registered account, because you will pay no tax, on any gains, until you sell. But stocks which do not pay a dividend will be Growth or Value stocks. Deciding which stocks will offer the greatest growth, trying to buy them at a reasonably low price, and deciding when to sell to preserve profits, is going back to market-watching and being concerned with market fluctuations. That's exactly what we want to avoid with our investments, at least I do. Instead, I want to buy stocks and then ignore price and the market. Income investing allows you to do just that. We also want income growth, because as the income grows, so will the value of your holdings.

However, since the dividends in a non-registered account are taxable, you should look to buy dividend growth stocks which have a history of offering a lower initial yield. You will end up receiving a smaller dividend, but a higher dividend growth history, which normally results in higher price gains. I have found there are not a lot of these types of stocks to choose from, but there will be a few. At this time, I will mention Canadian National Railway (CNR) and Metro Inc, (MRU) as examples. Normally, these two stocks are considered expensive when compared to other dividend growth stocks, but over the long-term these stocks will likely provide much higher capital growth. Capital gains are only taxed when you sell the stock and the tax on capital gains is much lower, even lower than the tax on dividends.

I do not suggest you buy any US stocks for a non-registered account as there is a 15% withholding tax on the dividends received, as well as tax on the balance of the dividend amount.

Chapter 3

The "Brass Tacks" of Income Investing

"The most important, fundamental, basic, or immediate facts, priorities, or realities of a situation". (Definition)

Do you understand Yield?

You may have found that I speak of, and use the word, "yield" often in describing my strategy and evaluation process. Yield is simply a measurement used to assist you with making decisions and measuring performance. There is Current Yield, Average Yield, Yield Difference and Percentage Change in the Yield. Each serves a different purpose or can be used with other forms of measurements to help you decide which stock has potential to buy and when, and aids you in evaluating your purchased stocks to see how they're doing. But in order to understand the importance of yield in your decision-making, you should know the different ways yield is defined in relation to stocks:

Current yield is simply the current annual dividend divided by the current price.

Average yield is the average yield over a specified period. This could be 10 years or more.

Yield difference is the difference between the Current yield and the Average yield.

Percentage yield change is the change in the yield from one year to the next.

Yield can be both simple and complex to calculate, depending on the information and figures you use and the frequency that you do your calculations. For example, how you determine the long-term Average Yield for a company can be calculated in multiple ways:

1. With my strategy, I record the yield once a year and then calculate the 10-year average.
2. Tom Connolly, my mentor, used to record the yield at the end of each

week, then calculate the average yield over an extended period.
3. Some calculate the yield monthly, then calculate the 10-year average.

If you calculated the 10-year average yield of a stock, using each of the above scenarios, one would get a slightly different 10-year average yield figure every time. But I don't believe the difference between the three calculations will make a big difference when applied to stock purchasing decisions.

The purpose of calculating a 10-year average yield is to have a measurement by which to compare the current yield. Keep in mind that the current yield of a stock changes as the price of the stock changes, which means it changes during the trading day, week and month. So, even if the 10-year average yield is not an exact figure, comparing the two figures still has meaning. We don't need exact figures to arrive at a reasonable conclusion.

To further illustrate this point, here are the yield charts of three communication stocks. These are Tom Connolly's, taken from his website and are based on weekly yield figures:

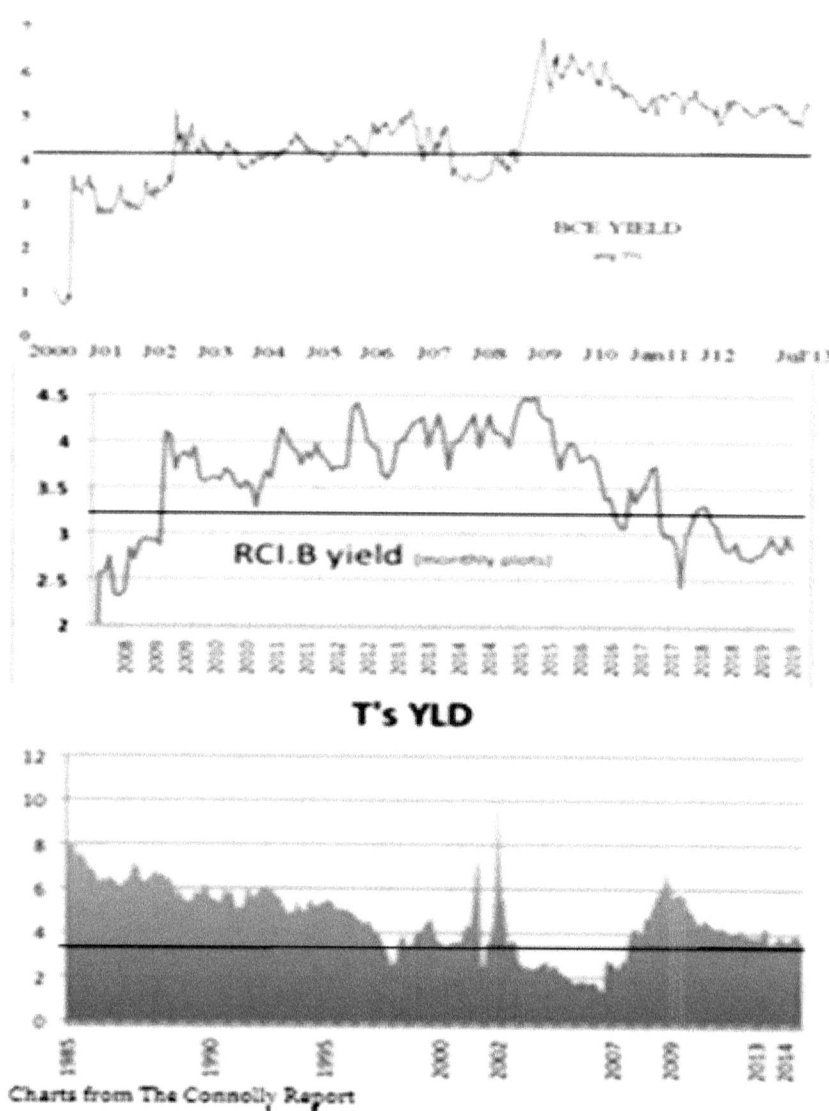

Charts from The Connolly Report

The charts above, (blurry as they are), show the yields over approximately 20 years, with BCE averaging about 4.1% yield, Rogers about 3.25% and Telus about 3.35%. Looking at the following chart, which calculates the 10-year average yield on a yearly basis for the three companies, the 10-year yields for the

Symbol	Company Name	10-Year Ave Yield calculated Weekly	10-Year Ave Yield calculated Yearly	Yield Difference
BCE	BCE Communications	4.10%	4.38%	0.28%
RCI-A	Rogers Communications	3.25%	3.43%	0.18%
T	Telus	3.35%	3.74%	0.39%

three stocks have slightly different figures.

The question is: does the yield difference, calculated weekly or yearly, to arrive at the 10-year average yield figures, make a difference in your decisions? Certainly, the more often you calculate the yield to determine a stock's long-term average, the more accurate the long-term average percentage will be. But I don't think the slight change in average yield figures will make a big difference in your analysis or decision making.

Take a look at two "Yield Difference" sample charts below:

Symbol	Company Name	Current Div	Current YLD %	10-Year Ave Yearly	Yield Difference	Current Price
BCE	BCE Comm	$3.33	5.87%	4.38%	1.49%	$56.75
T	Telus	$1.17	4.99%	3.74%	1.25%	$23.45
RCI-A	Rogers Comm	$2.00	3.34%	3.43%	-0.09%	$59.90

The 10-year average yield figures above are calculated using yearly yields for the three communication companies. Would the yield difference percentage change your opinion if we used the weekly 10-year averages, as shown below?

Symbol	Company Name	Current Div	Current YLD %	10-Year Ave Weekly	Yield Difference	Current Price
BCE	BCE Comm	$3.33	5.87%	4.10%	1.77%	$56.75
T	Telus	$1.17	4.99%	3.35%	1.64%	$23.45
RCI-A	Rogers Comm	$2.00	3.34%	3.25%	0.09%	$59.90

What I am trying to emphasize is that investing is not an exact science and so one must also look at your investment decisions subjectively. You don't need to have or know the exact figures when making financial decisions. Yes, you want to know the exact dividend paid and the correct dividend growth percentage, but when comparing that growth to a long-term average percentage, a reasonably close figure will do. But deciding whether the future dividend growth will continue as it has in the past cannot be accurately determined. You need to add your own opinion about the company, it's likelihood of continuing growth and the status of the company compared to others in the same sector. I think it's more important that whatever calculation you use to determine the long-term average yield, that you be consistent with your calculations, using the same measurement all the time.

Is it really Current Yield that matters?

Many believe that "what I get paid today is what really matters". When you purchase a stock or reinvest the dividend, you are paying the current price, so the yield is always *current yield* (current dividend divided by current price).

However, I prefer to concentrate on "Yield on Investment", which is the yield your entire portfolio provides (total dividends divided by total investment) and is different than current yield. Yield on investment is also not "Yield on Cost" (current dividend divided by original purchase price)", the difference can be illustrated by the following:

1. A stock pays a $3.60 dividend and the current price is $73.02, therefore the "Current yield" is 4.93% (3.60/73.02).
2. You invested $10,323 to buy the stock, mentioned in Point #1, 5 years ago, and it now pays $841.90 in dividends a year. The "Yield on Cost" is 8.15% (841.90/10,323).
3. Your total investment in this stock, mentioned in Point #2 (cost of all purchases and all reinvested dividends) is $14,470.23. The yearly dividends are $841.90, therefore "Yield on Investment" is 5.82% (841.90/14.471.23).

Each of the yield calculations provides different information and has a different meaning. The least important, at least to me, is the "Yield on Cost". In fact, most investors generally find this figure meaningless, or nothing but a feel-good figure.

As mentioned earlier, most investors feel the current yield is the most important measurement, but they also do not understand the Income investment strategy. Certainly, when you are looking at buying a stock today, the current yield is important. But new purchases will likely not be with large amounts of money, and will not be the larger part of your total investment. An investor's portfolio grows over time, not from a single purchase. So, your current purchases and reinvested dividends will only just slightly change your total yield on your entire portfolio.

With Income investing, <u>the yield on your total investment</u> should rise slowly and steadily over time.

Your yield on total investment rises because of:

- the yield on your purchases,
- the reinvested dividends,
- the dividend increases (and dividend cuts) and,
- because stock prices fluctuate.

It's the combined effect of all four that results in lowering the average cost of your investments and increasing your yield. The yield on your total investments will drop if one company cuts their dividend, but the overall yield may only drop slightly.

Once your investment gets to a certain level, your dividend reinvestments begin to contribute as much, if not more, to the growth of your portfolio and especially to the income your portfolio generates.

It is this "Rising Yield on Investment", of your entire portfolio, that determines how much income is generated and if you will reach the point of being able to live off the dividends (income). This rising yield tells you more than any other measurement. It tells you that you have invested in quality Income producing stocks. A rising yield also means you are earning more income on the money you have invested.

Let's look at an example. I have a Dividend Reinvestment account (DRIP), where I transferred shares of five companies into the account. The value of the five company shares, at the time of the transfer was $228,715.00. No additional funds were added and the dividends were not reinvested. The chart below shows Current Yield, the Yield on Cost, and the Yield on Total Investment, calculated each December 31st over five years:

Yield Comparison

	2015	2016	2017	2018	2019
Current Yield (Dec)	4.46%	4.25%	4.50%	4.79%	4.54%
Yield on Cost	5.70%	6.32%	6.99%	7.72%	8.58%
Yield on Investment	5.39%	5.94%	6.54%	7.16%	7.71%

· Current Yield is the average current yield of the five stocks at the end of December each year.

· Yield on Cost is calculated by dividing the current dividend paid by the average initial cost of the five stocks, at the end of each year. The rising percentage indicates that the companies must have raised their dividend in order for the yield to increase on the original purchase.

· Yield on Total Investment (recalculated with the dividends reinvested) calculates yield by dividing dividends received at the end of each year, from all five stocks, by the total amount invested (original cost, plus reinvested dividends). The rising percentage tells you that you are earning more income from your investment, as the percentage increases.

Current yield is only important if you are buying new shares or when dividends are reinvested.

Yield on Cost normally serves no purpose, but as the dividends from these five stocks are deposited into my bank, the rising yield on cost tells me the companies have raised their dividend and I'm receiving more income each year.

Yield on Total Investment is a real and meaningful figure. If the yield on total investment is a rising percentage, it tells you that you are earning more money for every dollar you invested. The percentage growth also means you will need less money invested to reach your future income goal.

Using yield to make purchase decisions

The stock evaluation process, described in my earlier books, was intended to guide you in developing your "List of Stocks to Consider". The stocks on your list are the ones you'll choose from when you decide to invest in stocks. Naturally, the next question is how do you decide which stocks to buy, and when?

By now, if you have learned anything about me, you will know that I think Excel spreadsheets are vital to my process. In both of my previous books I use Excel throughout to help with the recording and evaluation of stocks.

I have prepared a new Excel worksheet styled after "Tom Connolly's List" report, where he sorts his stock list by yield difference. My worksheet is called "Yield Difference" (surprise) and it will be used to sort the stocks on your list, from under-valued to expensive.

As discussed in my other books, one measure to determine if a stock is under-valued or expensive is to compare the current dividend yield to the stocks 10-year average dividend yield.

For the more experienced investor, feel free to include other test criteria or comparative data to help you decide when a stock is under-valued or expensive. Either way, I believe you will find that comparing current yield to the 10-year average yield will give you a good indication if the stocks are good buys or expensive. Certainly, it will indicate if you will obtain a reasonable income from your purchase, which is key to the Income investing process.

Yield Difference Worksheet

The "Yield Difference" worksheet will be the tool you use to assist you in deciding which stocks to buy and when. The worksheet will allow you to sort the stocks listed on the worksheet from under-valued, reasonably-priced, and expensive after entering the current price for each stock.

You can download the "Yield Difference" Excel worksheet from the following site:
https://drive.google.com/drive/folders/1kD-ZtK7WkIINobzB3HYJ1tnwnh9P3NDf?usp=sharing

If you have difficulty accessing the site, email me and I will send you a copy: **HMyourgrowingincome@gmail.com**

Let me explain that the terms "under-valued", "reasonably-priced" and "expensive" are not fixed. The worksheet simply shows the current yield difference when compared to the 10-year average yield for each stock.

· **"Under-valued"** are stocks whose current dividend yield is above their 10-year average dividend yield. At the high end, the yield difference would range from 1% to 3%. Any percentage above 3% should be viewed suspiciously, unless the stock market has crashed and the stock price has plummeted.

· **"Reasonably-priced"** stocks will be those where the current yield is close to their 10-year average yield for the stock. The range difference will vary and be dependent upon the yields of the other stocks in the same sector on your list.

· **"Expensive"** stocks would be those stocks whose current yield is below their 10-year average yield. The most expensive will show minus yield differences from the 10-year average.

It's the change of stock prices and whether the dividend paid changes, which causes the yield difference percentage to change. The stocks which appear at the top, after sorting, will be the under-valued ones, the ones in the middle will be reasonably priced, and the ones at the bottom will be the expensive ones.

There will be times when no stock will show a yield difference above 1% or even 2% above their 10-year average yield, while at other times some might be above 3%.

I will describe here the process to determine a stock's yield difference using an Excel worksheet:

1. Open the "Yield Difference" Excel worksheet.
2. Click on the "CdnYldDif" tab at the bottom.

Symbol	Canadian Company Name	Current Div	Current YLD%	10-Yr Ave Yield	Yield Difference	Current Price	Declared Div Mo
ACO-X	Atco Ltd., Cl.I,	1.74	4.76%		4.76%	36.58	M/J/S/D
ADW-A	Andrew Peller Ltd.	0.22	2.46%		2.46%	8.76	M/J/S/D
ATD-B	Alimentation Couche-Tard Inc	0.00	#DIV/0!		#DIV/0!		M/J/S/D
BAM-A	Brookfield Asset Management Inc	0.00	#DIV/0!		#DIV/0!		F/M/A/N
BCE	BCE Inc	0.00	#DIV/0!		#DIV/0!		M/A/N/F

tabs: 45 Cdn Stks | Cdn DivGth% | CdnYldDif | UsYldDif | US Di...

All 45 Canadian dividend growth stocks will be listed.

1. Because this template lists all 45 Canadian stocks, you should delete those stocks which did not make your "List of Stocks to Consider". (To delete: Left click the row number on the left side of the worksheet to highlight the row, then right click and left click "Delete".)
2. You can add other stocks to your list if desired. Don't worry if they are not listed alphabetically. You can and will be sorting them later.
3. Each stock should include the following information:

- Stock symbol
- Stock name
- 10-year average yield
- Current annual dividend amount

1. Calculate the 10-year average yield for each stock on your list, as described in my earlier books. Once you have calculated the 10-year average, you're done. You don't need to re-calculate the figure, unless

you wish to update the figure at the end of the next year.

1. Ensure that the current annual dividend amount for each stock listed is the correct amount. (There are online sources available to retrieve this information that I will discuss later.)
2. As you enter a different dividend amount, the current yield will automatically be calculated, based on the current price amount shown.
3. Enter the current stock market price for all the stocks on your list. You may find it easier to set up a stock portfolio with information from a site like Yahoo Finance for the stocks on your list (which will be discussed a bit later).
4. The next step will be to sort the stocks by the "Yield Dif" column.
5. Block all the relevant columns on the worksheet (i.e.: A to G.) Left click and hold the left mouse button on column A, then move the mouse button to column G and release the mouse button. All columns should be highlighted.
6. Next, click on the tab "Data" at the top.

7. Click on the "Sort" box as shown above.

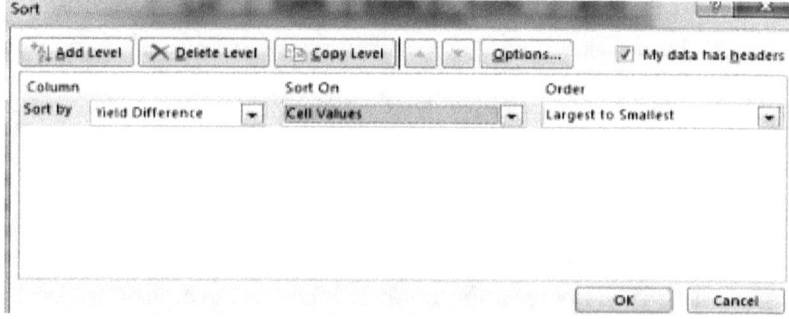

8.

INCOME INVESTING EXPLAINED

Set the choices as shown below:

1. Click the down arrow for the "Sort by" option and select "Yield Difference", and set the "Order" to "Largest to Smallest".
2. Click "OK".
3. The worksheet will then list the stocks by order of the highest yield difference down to the lowest yield difference. The small sample below shows the list before and after being sorted.

Before Sorted:

Symbol	Canadian Company Name	Current Div	Current YLD%	10-Yr Ave Yield	Yield Difference	Current Price	Declared Div Mo
ACO-X	Atco Ltd., Cl I.	1.74	4.10%	1.60%	2.50%	42.43	J/A/J/O
ADW-A	Andrew Peller Ltd.	0.22	2.57%	2.34%	0.23%	8.38	M/J/S/D
ATD-B	Alimentation Couche	0.28	0.60%	0.35%	0.25%	46.39	J/A/J/O
BAM-A	Brookfield Asset Mgt	0.48	1.02%	1.18%	-0.16%	46.91	M/J/S/D
BCE	BCE	3.33	5.78%	4.87%	0.91%	57.58	M/J/S/D

After Sorted:

Symbol	Canadian Company Name	Current Div	Current YLD%	10-Yr Ave Yield	Yield Difference	Current Price	Declared Div Mo
ACO-X	Atco Ltd., Cl I.	1.74	4.10%	1.60%	2.50%	42.43	J/A/J/O
BCE	BCE	3.33	5.78%	4.87%	0.91%	57.58	M/J/S/D
ATD-B	Alimentation Couche	0.28	0.60%	0.35%	0.25%	46.39	J/A/J/O
ADW-A	Andrew Peller Ltd.	0.22	2.57%	2.34%	0.23%	8.38	M/J/S/D
BAM-A	Brookfield Asset Mgt	0.48	1.02%	1.18%	-0.16%	46.91	M/J/S/D

1. Save the worksheet to your computer or storage drive, make sure to rename the worksheet file (I'd suggest using the date you entered the data, for instance, "Yield Difference Jul22").
2. You may wish to print out the worksheet and refer to it later for a quick comparison, to see how the stocks on your list move up and down in position over time. I find this useful to get a quick snapshot of which stocks are currently under-valued and reasonably priced.
3. Keep the Canadian and US stocks on a separate worksheet.
4. The stocks at the top of the "Yield Difference" worksheet, with the largest yield difference, will be considered less expensive or possibly under-valued, while the ones at the bottom will be more expensive.

1. If you wish to sort the stocks alphabetically, repeat the "Sort" process described above: block all the columns (i.e.: A to G), select "Symbol", rather than "Yield Difference" and set the "Order" to "A to Z".

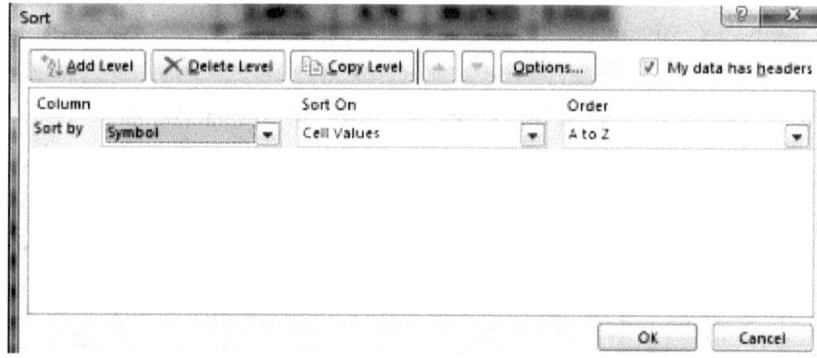

The "Yield Difference" worksheet is your buying guide, indicating which stocks on your list are offering a higher dividend yield than their 10-year average dividend yield. The higher the yield difference, the cheaper the stock is at the current market price.

The "Yield Difference" worksheet is used in conjunction with the "Dividend Growth" worksheet in determining which stock you should consider purchasing. I will provide an example of the process later in the book.

Further Explanation of the "Yield Difference" Worksheet:

Symbol	Canadian Company Name	Current Div	Current YLD%	10-Yr Ave Yield	Yield Difference	Current Price	Declared Div Mo
ACO-X	Atco Ltd., Cl.I.	1.74	4.10%	1.60%	2.50%	42.43	J/A/J/O
BCE	BCE	3.33	5.78%	4.87%	0.91%	57.58	M/J/S/D
ATD-B	Alimentation Couche	0.28	0.60%	0.35%	0.25%	46.39	J/A/J/O
ADW-A	Andrew Peller Ltd.	0.22	2.57%	2.34%	0.23%	8.38	M/J/S/D
BAM-A	Brookfield Asset Mgt	0.48	1.02%	1.18%	-0.16%	46.91	M/J/S/D

1. The "Yield Difference" column in the "Yield Difference" worksheet shows the percentage difference between the current yield and the 10-year average yield.
2. Stocks whose current yield is above the 10-year average yield (1% or higher) are considered under-valued.
3. Stocks with a current yield below the 10-average (especially with a negative difference) are considered expensive.
4. The stocks whose current yield is close to, or just above the 10-year average yield, may be considered reasonably-priced.
5. Under normal market conditions, when the market is stable or growing steadily, you would like to buy stocks which have a yield difference above their 10-year average yield. But if the market and stock prices are rising, you may have to settle for those offering a yield closer to or equal to the 10-year average.
6. Stocks which show a negative yield difference indicate that the price of the stock is high, and this would likely discourage you from buying them at that time.
7. Normally you will compare the yield difference of stocks within the same sector, for instance, all the banks or all utilities, when choosing to buy a stock in a particular sector.
8. When a stock has a large yield difference above the 10-year average, it is offering the lowest price and possibly the most income for your invested dollars. However, if the yield difference is extremely high,

3% or more above its 10-year average, proceed with some caution. You may need to investigate why the price of the stock has dropped and what has caused this yield difference, and then decide if the dividend is safe.
- Might the company have run into debt?
- Has something in the economy affected the company and the price has dropped?
- Did the company miss its expected quarterly earnings or revenue forecasts?
- Did the market have a correction and did all stock prices drop?

    a. Based on a review of a stock, you will have to ask if you believe the large yield difference will result in a dividend cut, or will the company be able to meet its dividend obligation.
    b. Do you feel the company has sufficient free cash-flow to meet the dividend, even if earnings are low and the payout ratio high?
    c. The real concern is if the company might have to cut the dividend.
    d. For most quality dividend growth stocks, they normally will not cut the dividend, except under exceptional circumstances.
    e. Even if you believe the company might continue to pay the dividend, do you feel they will continue to increase the dividend as they have in the past? Normally, quality dividend companies raise their dividend on specific quarters each year.

9. Always keep in mind that you are using your "List of Stocks to Consider" and the yield difference to decide which stocks to buy and when you believe they are safe.

Under normal or rising market conditions, a conservative income investor might not wish to buy the stocks with the largest yield difference. More likely, they will consider buying stocks from the list which are just below the ones with the highest yield difference. Stocks with the highest yield difference may

INCOME INVESTING EXPLAINED

be those with current financial difficulty or have been affected by economic factors.

The old saying "better safe than sorry", might be appropriate when you are unsure of why the yield difference is so high.

The stocks just below the highest yield difference stocks, will likely be those that offer a safe dividend at a reasonable price. The stocks closer to the bottom will offer the safest dividend, but at a higher price.

The Buying Trap

We've all done it; bought a stock which offered an enticing dividend yield of 6% to 7%, where the company has paid and raised its dividend for a number of years, and we believe the dividend will be safe. Remember, stocks which offer a higher initial yield, will also be the ones which offer a lower dividend growth rate. During good times, when the market is rising, they will likely continue to be a good dividend producer. But as soon as there is a market correction, watch out. Once the dividend yield rises, especially going above 10% the likelihood of a dividend cut is almost a certainty. **Don't risk a dividend cut, just for the sake of a slightly higher initial yield.**

Let's look at three initial stock yields, and add an expected dividend growth rate, to arrive at a projected dividend return.

1. Higher initial yield (6% to 7%), but lower dividend growth rate:

6% initial yield, plus 3% to 4% growth = 9% to 10% Total dividend growth.

1. Average initial yield (3.5% to 5%) with an average dividend growth rate:

4% initial yield, plus 5% to 8% growth = 9% to 12% Total dividend growth

1. Lower initial yield (.025% to 2.0%), with a higher dividend growth rate:

1% initial yield, plus 12% to 14% growth = 13% to 15% Total dividend growth.

Your long-term income growth will be the total of the initial yield plus the dividend growth percentage.

If the three examples above appear realistic, then all three will offer between 10% to 15% income growth over the long-term. But you must consider which will be the safest to invest in. It should make sense that the "safest" dividend stocks will be the ones that offer a lower initial yield, because the likelihood of a dividend cut will be lower. Less certain will be the ability of a company to maintain a higher dividend growth rate. But it should also make sense that an average growth rate should be more sustainable than a high growth rate.

I suggest you protect yourself from a possible dividend cut by looking beyond the initial yield, and include the potential growth your income provides when you have funds to invest. Those 6% and higher initial yields are tempting, but much less safe than an initial 3% to 5% yield, and when you add a realistic dividend growth rate of 5% to 8% a year, your future income growth is almost guaranteed.

Remember, during market corrections, one can live without a dividend increase but not a dividend cut.

The Yahoo Finance portfolio

The Yahoo Finance website is an example of an online source for stock information. You can easily set up a list of stocks you wish to monitor and obtain current stock prices.

To access their information, you will go to the Yahoo finance website, register and setup your logon information. Once you've registered you can then set up a stock portfolio list.

INCOME INVESTING EXPLAINED

Symbol	Last Price	Change	Chg %	Currency
ACO-X.TO	37.48	-0.19	-0.50%	CAD
ADW-A.TO	9.11	-0.02	-0.22%	CAD
BAM-A.TO	46.42	+0.65	+1.42%	CAD
BCE.TO	56.54	-0.39	-0.69%	CAD
BIP-UN.TO	54.56	+0.07	+0.13%	CAD
BMO.TO	67.10	-0.88	-1.29%	CAD

https://ca.finance.yahoo.com/

Whenever you access the website and click on "My Portfolio", your stocks will be shown with a variety of useful information. By clicking on "Symbol", the stocks will be sorted alphabetically.

In my book, *Your Ever Growing Income*, I provide many different online sources for stock information. I feel quite strongly that the more information we have access to as investors the more confident we can become in making independent and informed decisions when purchasing stock.

Finding a company's CurrentDividend

In order for your "Yield Difference" Excel worksheet comparison to be valid, you need to know the current annual dividend of each company on your list. The most accurate information is obtained from the company's website or annual reports, but this can be time consuming and difficult to compile, especially if you are tracking a large number of stocks.

One of the best sites I can recommend to obtain current dividend data can be found at the **Dividend History** website.

https://dividendhistory.org/

Upon visiting this site, you can enter the company "symbol" to see the dividend data.

Below is a screen shot from the website of a dividend Fortis recently paid. You can search dividends paid back to at least 15

Dividend History		Dividend Calendar	Dividend Reports	Dividend Announcements
Fortis (FTS)		Frequency: Quarterly (multipy by 4 to obtain yearly dividend)		
Ex-Dividend Date	Payout Date	Cash Amount	% Change	
11/17/2020	11/30/2020	$0.4775**	unconfirmed/estimated	
8/18/2020	8/31/2020	$0.4775**	unconfirmed/estimated	
5/14/2020	6/1/2020	$0.48		
2/14/2020	3/1/2020	$0.48		
11/18/2019	12/1/2019	$0.48	6.11% Increase	
8/19/2019	9/1/2019	$0.45		

years.

In the sample above you will see that Fortis is currently paying a $0.48 quarterly dividend, so you will multiply 0.48 x 4 and record $1.92 as the current dividend amount on the "Yield Difference" worksheet.

INCOME INVESTING EXPLAINED 59

You can also record the months that the dividends are paid so you'll know when the next dividend is due on the "Yield Difference" worksheet. You will enter the annual dividend amounts, as shown below:

Symbol	Canadian Company Name	Current Div	Current YLD%	10-Yr Ave Yield	Yield Difference	Current Price	Declared Div Mo
ACO-X	Atco Ltd., Cl.I.	1.74	4.10%	1.60%	2.50%	42.43	J/A/J/O
BCE	BCE	3.33	5.78%	4.87%	0.91%	57.58	M/J/S/D
ATD-B	Alimentation Couche	0.28	0.60%	0.35%	0.25%	46.39	J/A/J/O
ADW-A	Andrew Peller Ltd.	0.22	2.57%	2.34%	0.23%	8.38	M/J/S/D
BAM-A	Brookfield Asset Mgt	0.48	1.02%	1.18%	-0.16%	46.91	M/J/S/D

At the "Home" screen, or if you click on the "Dividend Announcement" tab on the site, you will see notifications of companies which have raised, cut or changed the frequency of

2020-06-02	UNH	United Health Group raises dividend 15.7% to $1.25 quarterly
2020-06-01	LB	Laurentian Bank cuts dividend 40% to $0.40 quarterly
2020-06-01	OXY	Occidental Petroleum cuts dividend 99% to $0.01 quarterly
2020-05-28	CMG	Computer Modelling Group cuts dividend 50% to $0.05 quarterly
2020-05-21	HAL	Halliburton cuts dividend 75% to $0.045 quarterly
2020-05-21	NOC	Northrop Grumman raises dividend 10% to $1.45 quarterly
2020-05-18	LNF	Leons Furniture cuts dividend 25% to $0.12 quarterly

their dividend:

This information shows which companies are raising or cutting their dividend. It's unfortunate that they don't provide access to past monthly data for dividend increases and cuts.

Finding under-valued stocks in rising markets

When markets are rising, as they did from 2009 to 2020 (with a slight dip in 2016), it seems difficult to find under-valued stocks. Everyone stresses the importance of buying when stocks are low and not when they are expensive or over-valued.

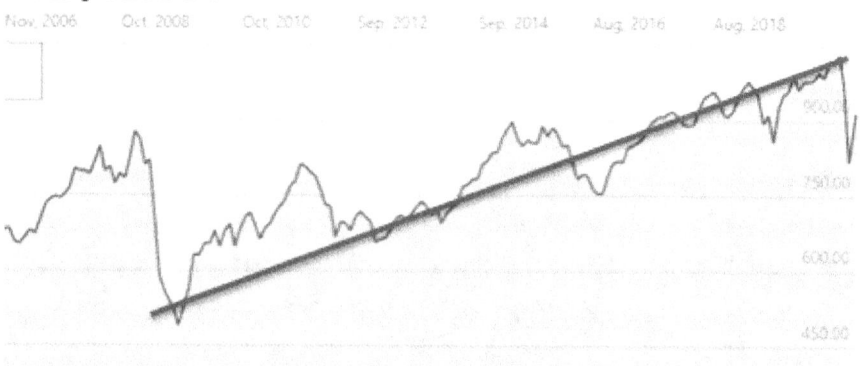

It has been suggested that you should hold on to your cash and to be prepared to buy should the market dip or if there is a correction. I have even been known to say it myself. But is holding cash, waiting for the best time to buy really that necessary?

When you are just starting to invest you might not have much money to buy stocks. Or perhaps you want to start out slowly before you invest more than you are comfortable with. Investors would like to avoid the high cost of commissions, so try to save up to at least $1,000 before making a buy. Most stocks cost between $30 to $100 a share, so you could buy between 10 to 30 shares with a $1,000 purchase. There are many reasons, including a rising market, that factor into whether to start buying stocks. But I argue that with Income investing, the sooner you can get started the better, regardless of how the market is performing.

I've suggested that under-valued stocks are those whose current yield is higher than the 10-year average yield of the stock. That's your starting point. Use your "Yield Difference" worksheet to look for those under-valued stocks. But don't restrict yourself just to those which are under-valued by yield.

INCOME INVESTING EXPLAINED

When prices are rising quickly, as in a bull market, you may have difficulty finding under-valued stocks. This is when you should remember that reasonable yields should not be over looked. If you can find stocks which offer yields close to their 10-year average, these may still be good stocks to buy. What you don't want to do is buy those where the current yields are well below the 10-year average yields.

If you can get a reasonable yield, then get your money invested and working to increase your income. Holding off for a fraction of a percentage increase, might seem prudent, but how much more income will you gain and how long might you have to wait, before you can buy at a better price? No one knows what the market will do, and this difference is hardly a reason to wait. I recommend that you just go ahead and buy when you have sufficient funds and try to buy at a reasonable price or yield. There is no time like the present to start earning income! Look at the quarterly prices in the chart below. They go from a low of $42 to a high of $54, and continued to rise slowly, until the health crisis hit. We can't know when prices might drop, so settle for a good stock at a reasonable price or yield.

MAR 29\18	42.8000	1.8633	79.75
JUN 28\18	42.1956	1.9090	80.55
SEP 27\18	42.0093	1.9367	81.36
DEC 31\18	44.4200	1.9588	87.01
MAR 29\19	49.7600	1.7665	87.90
JUN 28\19	52.6624	1.6841	88.69
SEP 27\19	56.1501	1.5931	89.45
DEC 31\19	54.2600	1.7634	95.68
MAR 29\20	44.5400	2.1670	96.52
JUN 28\20	52.1348	1.8711	97.55

The point is, don't get hung up on trying to find or buy when stocks are only under-valued. If your investment timeframe is at least 10 years or longer, dollar cost averaging will get you where you wish to go. Dollar cost averaging is buying more shares when prices are low and less when prices are high. That is the key to the Income Growth Investment Strategy: invest regularly, buy stocks which offer a reasonable yield, reinvest the dividends, and if possible, add more funds during market corrections. Earning income is the goal, and market-watching does not determine success or failure.

Which stocks do I like?

This is one of the questions I get asked most often, and I understand why. Having followed Income Investing for years, some might feel I know which are the good stocks to buy. Normally, I don't give an answer or I give a general statement, *"I always try to find the stock with the best yield in the sector I'm interested in".* Trust me, I can see why this might be frustrating to some. I can literally hear the person grumbling *"Thanks a Lot!"*

But it's really the best answer I can give. Stock prices fluctuate daily, companies' status may change at any time, and choosing a stock involves a lot of different decisions, influenced by everyone's different perspectives. I have always stressed that people should learn how to assess stocks themselves using widely available information. Even if we all come to make the same choices in the end, I think it's best that the investor understands why that choice is best for them.

To demonstrate this point, let's look at three stocks, but in the same sector. If you wish to buy a stock in a specific sector, like Communications, then compare the data of the stocks you have listed in that sector. Try to get a feel for which might offer:

1. The most reasonable or best current dividend yield.
2. The best 10-year dividend growth history.
3. The best maintained year-to-year dividend growth.
4. The one that seems to be the strongest, and therefore, has the safest dividend in the near future.

Let's consider three of the largest communications companies in Canada for comparison: Bell (BCE), Rogers (RCI) and Telus (T). You could invest in all three, but I prefer to do an evaluation and hopefully end up picking the one(s) that is currently the best of the best.

INCOME INVESTING EXPLAINED

BCE	2010	2011	2012	2013	2014	2015	2016	2017	2018	2019	Gth/Yld
Dividend	1.78	2.04	2.22	2.33	2.47	2.60	2.73	2.87	3.02	3.17	78.09%
% Chg		14.61%	8.82%	4.95%	6.01%	5.26%	5.00%	5.13%	5.23%	4.97%	
Price	36.37	40.88	44.31	46.76	56.36	56.43	58.66	57.52	57.13	62.36	10yrAve%
Yield %	4.89%	4.99%	5.01%	4.98%	4.38%	4.61%	4.65%	4.99%	5.29%	5.08%	4.89%

RCI.B	2010	2011	2012	2013	2014	2015	2016	2017	2018	2019	Gth/Yld
Dividend	1.28	1.42	1.58	1.74	1.83	1.92	1.92	1.92	1.92	2.00	56.25%
% Chg		10.94%	11.27%	10.13%	5.17%	4.92%	0.00%	0.00%	0.00%	4.17%	
Price	36.50	39.21	46.91	47.79	47.40	47.78	57.12	60.10	71.00	66.91	10yrAve%
Yield %	3.51%	3.62%	3.37%	3.64%	3.86%	4.02%	3.36%	3.19%	2.70%	2.99%	3.43%

T	2010	2011	2012	2013	2014	2015	2016	2017	2018	2019	Gth/Yld
Dividend	0.50	0.55	0.55	0.61	0.68	0.76	0.84	0.92	0.98	1.05	110.00%
% Chg		10.00%	0.00%	10.91%	11.48%	11.76%	10.53%	9.52%	6.52%	7.14%	
Price	12.41	14.13	16.85	19.47	21.80	19.49	21.72	23.16	23.01	26.52	10yrAve%
Yield %	4.03%	3.89%	3.26%	3.13%	3.12%	3.90%	3.87%	3.97%	4.26%	3.96%	3.74%

We will be using our Excel worksheets to help us determine which might be the ideal stock of the three. The above chart summarizes the "Dividend Growth" worksheets for each, highlights the 10-year dividend growth and the last few year-to-year dividend percentages.

1. Review the dividend paid during the past 10 years for each.
2. Look for an increase in the dividend over the 10-year period.
3. Calculate the 10-year average dividend growth, remember that you're looking for at least 75% growth.
4. Calculate the year-to-year percentage change in the dividend over the previous years.
5. Ensure that the year-to-year dividend growth has not fallen below 3% for the last few years. If it has, this indicates a problem.

Compare the results of each. Remember you are comparing the data with other stocks in the same sector because you are trying to determine which company might continue to provide good dividend growth in the near future. Reported news on the companies or industry, growth in subscribers, expansion plans, or just your personal opinion of each may be relevant to any decisions you will be making. These markers are the first things you'll look at when deciding which to buy.

When we looked at the 10-year dividend history, the year-to-year dividend percentages and the 10-year dividend growth for each company (from the previous chart), Telus appears to be the best of the three, with Rogers coming in third.

Now look at the "Yield Difference" chart below, BCE is offering the highest yield difference, showing 1.43% above its 10-year average yield. Telus has a 1.38% yield difference and Rogers is showing a negative 0.09% yield difference.

Symbol	Company Name	Current Div	Current YLD %	10-Year Ave Yield	Yield Difference	Current Price
BCE	BCE Comm	$3.33	5.87%	4.38%	1.49%	$56.75
T	Telus	$1.17	5.12%	3.74%	1.38%	$22.85
RCI-A	Rogers Comm	$2.00	3.34%	3.43%	-0.09%	$59.90

Which stock would I buy of the three? At this time, I'd pick Telus then BCE. BCE and Telus offer a reasonably high initial yield, with Rogers' yield below its 10-year average. If you review the "Dividend Growth" worksheet, Telus seems to offer a higher past dividend growth rate and has maintained its dividend growth. Also, Telus has maintained a higher year-to year dividend growth rate.

You have to review the data, do the comparisons, decide which stock you like the best in that particular sector, and choose the one which you feel offers the best chance of continuing to grow their dividend going forward. The decision should always be up to you.

Sometimes it's easy to choose, other times you may wish to invest in more than one stock, or even decide that you might be better off looking at a different sector altogether. The nice thing is that you don't have to start from scratch, you already know which stocks to consider, don't you?

Maybe instead of asking which stocks I like we should take a look at those I don't like. And those are any stock which might be categorized as **cyclical**. These include energy, auto, airline, mining, housing, transportation, some durable and soft goods. I won't name specific companies as there are too many to include here, but you get the idea.

I think it is better to stick with large, established and mature companies which have proven that they have, and can, survive most economic and political upheavals. They will be those "Steady-Eddies" which have paid and raised their dividend consistently year after year. Most of the ones I like are included in the 45 Canadian and 35 US dividend growth stocks, listed in Appendix A and B. That's another reason I have included them in this book as a starting point for your review.

Why is reinvesting dividends so important?

I've covered this topic extensively in my other books, but I believe it is important enough to repeat here. It's my opinion that you should **reinvest your dividends every chance you get!**

Whether your broker offers only a synthetic DRIP, which allows you to only buy full shares, or full dividend reinvestment where you would be able to buy fractions of shares, **reinvest the dividends!** I cannot emphasize enough the importance of dividend reinvestment because of the compounding effect it will have on your future income growth.

Many investors prefer to let the dividends collect in their brokers account and add money for future purchases. Their reasoning is that they prefer to select which stocks to buy with the money and the freedom to buy a stock which will offer a better yield. When you select to reinvest the dividends, you only invest in the same stock, don't get to decide the price you will pay or when shares will be bought.

With automatic dividend reinvestment, you will buy more shares when the market is down and less when it's up. Over the long-term your purchases will average below the current market price. This method, as mentioned, is commonly referred to as "dollar cost averaging".

The other point to remember, is that the dividend will not likely be in large amounts, at least during the early accumulation phase of your investment. So why not buy as many shares as you can, at no cost.

Even if the dividend received is a significant amount, reinvest. I receive more than $3,000 from one stock each quarter and I still use dividend reinvestment. Yes, I could find a stock offering a better yield, but then I'd have to take the time and effort to search or it. With full dividend reinvestment, a lot of the work is done for you.

In conclusion, I don't think there's much point in watching the market on pins and needles for the absolute best time and price to buy. Time wasted in my opinion that is better spent accruing interest and income.

It may be easier to see the benefits of Income investing and dividend reinvestment using a very real investment option offered to Canadians, the Tax Free Savings Account (TFSA).

The following is an updated chart from my first book, *Your Ever Growing Income*. The chart shows me and my wife's TFSA accounts, the dividends received, reinvested, and how the yield on our total investment has grown over time.

Hm TFSA	Original Investment	Dividend Income	Div % Gth	Original plus Div	Accumulated investment	Yield on Investment
2009	5,000.00	144.94		5,144.94	5,144.94	2.82%
2010	5,000.00	399.00	175.29%	5,399.00	10,543.94	3.78%
2011	5,000.00	862.35	116.13%	5,862.35	16,406.29	5.26%
2012	5,000.00	959.70	11.29%	5,959.70	22,365.99	4.29%
2013	5,500.00	1313.46	36.86%	6,813.46	29,179.45	4.50%
2014	5,500.00	1742.35	32.65%	7,242.35	36,421.80	4.78%
2015	10,000.00	2404.75	38.02%	12,404.75	48,826.55	4.93%
2016	5,500.00	3301.78	37.30%	8,801.78	57,628.33	5.73%
2017	5,500.00	3813.66	15.50%	9,313.66	66,941.99	5.70%
2018	5,500.00	4574.95	19.96%	10,074.95	77,016.94	5.94%
2019	6,000.00	5551.15	21.34%	11,551.15	88,568.09	6.27%

Rm TFSA	Original Investment	Dividend Income	Div % Gth	Original plus Div	Accumulated investment	Yield on Investment
2009	5,000.00	129.82		5,129.82	5,129.82	2.53%
2010	5,000.00	399.00	207.35%	5,399.00	10,528.82	3.79%
2011	5,000.00	758.17	90.02%	5,758.17	16,286.99	4.66%
2012	5,000.00	1,116.20	47.22%	6,116.20	22,403.19	4.98%
2013	5,500.00	1,516.00	35.82%	7,016.00	29,419.19	5.15%
2014	5,500.00	2,182.03	43.93%	7,682.03	37,101.22	5.88%
2015	10,000.00	2,917.74	33.72%	12,917.74	50,018.96	5.83%
2016	5,500.00	3,661.32	25.48%	9,161.32	59,180.28	6.19%
2017	5,500.00	4,143.28	13.16%	9,643.28	68,823.56	6.02%
2018	5,500.00	5,060.57	22.14%	10,560.57	79,384.13	6.37%
2019	6,000.00	5,704.57	12.73%	11,704.57	91,088.70	6.26%

You can see that we both contributed the total maximum allowed every year to 2019, for a total of $63,500.00. My accumulated dividends were $25,068 and my wife received $27,589, which were reinvested. It's the combination of the annual contributions, dividends, and any dividend increases which account for the rising "Div % Gth" and "Yield on Investment" percentages.

The maximum annual contributions were made at the beginning of each year, with no attempt to try and invest at the best price or even considering the yield of the stocks, in other words we used Dollar Cost Averaging. Yet the income from both accounts grew as did our yield on total investment. This investment period also included the financial crisis of 2008, its recovery and minor market dips over the past 11 years.

We shall continue to contribute the maximum allowed at the beginning of each year, reinvest the dividends and ignore the market. We expect our income will continue to grow as it has in the past, at a very reasonable rate. Check the last column of the chart and see the rising yield on investment percentage grow. How might you ask does this happen? In a single word: Compounding!

Just as a point of interest, I hold only four dividend growth stocks in my TFSA, while my wife has five stocks. I simply cannot extol the virtues of a TFSA enough, along with Income investing. I cannot believe anyone would not want to take advantage of this strategy!

Chapter 4

When is the best time to buy?

Everyone wants the answer to this question. And the commonly accepted answer is: the best time to buy is when stocks are cheap! But when are stocks really cheap? When the market crashes, but do we ever really know when a market crash will occur or how long it will last? And ultimately, most investors don't really want the market to go down, especially if they are investing for capital returns.

As remarkable or devastating as market crashes are, they don't actually happen that often. Over the past 40 years there have only been four major market corrections:

Early 1990s - The invasion of Iraq
2000 Dot-com bubble - Collapse of technology stocks
2008 Financial crisis - Worldwide financial crisis

2020 Covid-19 crisis - Global pandemic

There were smaller market corrections in between these events, but they were of much shorter duration and affected different countries and/or market sectors.

Often people "hold" onto their money, waiting for a perfect market to buy. I personally don't recommend holding onto cash, waiting for the next market correction. My investing goals have always been to invest when I had the funds, making sure to pay as small a commission as possible. Even then, commissions should not be a major concern, as you will probably not be trading that often. How often do you buy shares? Monthly, quarterly, or possibly only once or twice a year? Even if you end up paying $10 per trade and you invest a minimum of $1,000 each time, your commission only represents about 1% of that purchase. I have always tried to invest a minimum of $2,500 at a time, thereby reducing the trading commission to .40 of one percent.

In my previous books I've suggested that you should maintain a buy "price and yield range" for the stocks on your list. When the market has a correction, as in the current Covid-19 health crisis, prices will drop and yields will be much better when you set those yield ranges. Even if the market has risen from its low point, the yields should still be much higher than when the market was growing or stagnate. However, when there is a market correction or recession, the market will stay down for several months or longer.

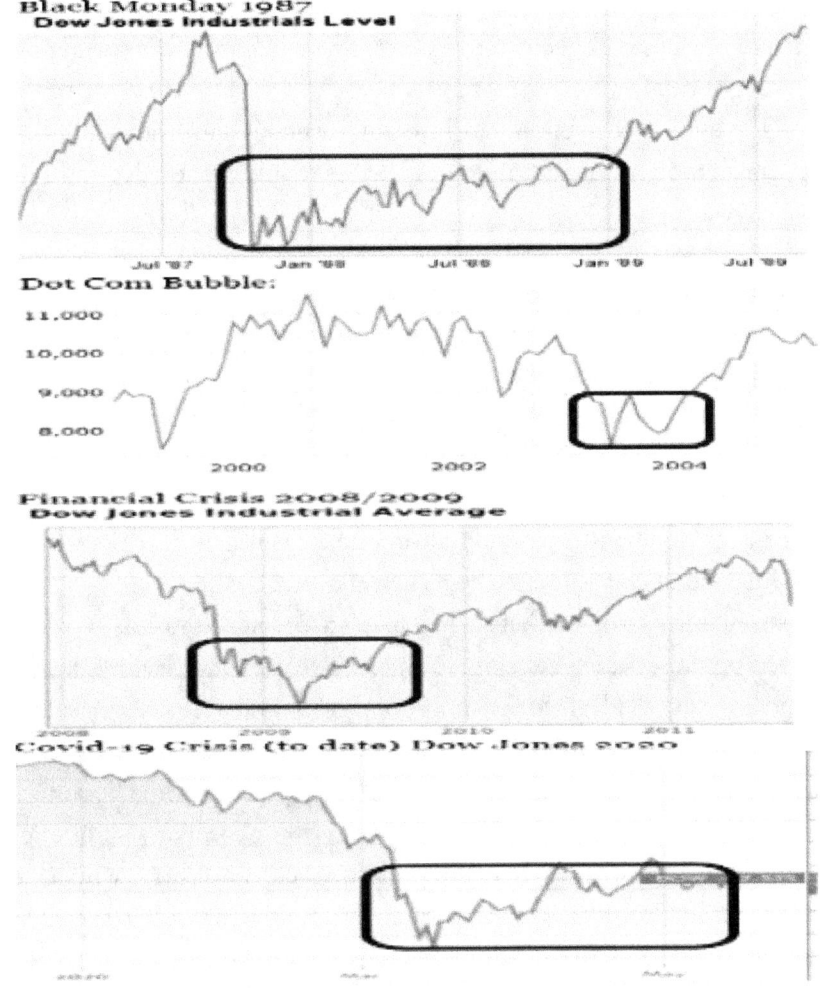

In the charts I have provided above, Ihave used the US Dow Jones charts, although the Canadian TSX Index charts would be similar. You may not be able to buy at the bottom price, but one would have had lots of opportunity to buy at prices 15% to 20% lower than before the market crashed. You don't need to buy just when the correction happens, there will be time, just be patient.

Some investors like holding onto 10% or more in cash reserves, in expectation of a market correction. It's a personal choice, but I feel there are several difficulties with holding cash:

1. No one has ever been able to determine when a market correction might occur.
2. The market correction may be of an extremely short duration, which means you probably would not be able to buy at the price you'd like anyway.

If you like the idea of holding some cash to buy at a much lower price, one option is to place a "Limit Order", a price you'd like to buy a specific stock at, perhaps 10% to 15% below the current price, and which offers a better yield. Be sure to set the expiry date for the "Limit Order" for at least a month and remind yourself to re-set the date if the order has not been filled.

During normal market conditions, when the market does not fluctuate very much but rises slowly, there should always be a few quality stocks which are under-valued when compared to their 10-year average yield.

However, during bull markets, when prices are rising almost daily, your best buys might be those which are close to their 10-year average yield. Usually you won't find a variety of ideal stocks, nor a good stock available in every sector. So if you do want to buy, don't worry if you only invest in a certain sector, or end up owning a large amount of a single stock. The only time I would be concerned about owning too many shares of one company is if the company is not one that you have decided is a quality dividend growth stock. And this is why having a "List of Stocks to Consider" is so important. When the market presents buying opportunities you can move much more quickly when you already have a list of vetted stocks to choose from.

In summary, the best time to buy is when you have the funds to invest.

If the markets are stable or rising you will look to those stocks which offer yields close to or just above the 10-year average yields. Should there be a market drop or correction, take advantage of the much higher yields, but don't worry if you don't get the lowest price. A 15% or 20% price drop will still provide a much higher yield than the 10-year average of most stocks. Remember, you are investing for the long-term.

Rather than trying to buy when stocks are cheap, I prefer to suggest you don't buy when stocks are expensive.

If you concentrate on the lowest price or the highest yield, you'll miss out on reasonably-priced stocks. Try to recognize when stocks are reasonably priced and offer a reasonable dividend yield. By doing so you'll easily identify the expensive stocks. Should conditions change and prices drop drastically, and you have the money, that's when you should jump on those cheap stocks.

Buying expensive stocks

Didn't I just suggest not buying expensive stocks? Well that's the rule but there is always the exception. When the market takes a nosedive and stays down, all stocks will drop in price and most will offer very tempting yields. But these are the times when you might wish to change your stock selection process a little.

I've suggested you use the "Yield Difference" Excel spreadsheet to determine under-valued and expensive stocks. Then use the information to buy those stocks which offer higher yields than their 10-year average yield. But during market crashes, you suddenly have the opportunity to buy shares of companies that you may have always considered too expensive. In the previous section I suggested you don't buy stocks when they are expensive, but each stock will have its own range of under-valued and expensive prices.

For example, let's say you were interested in buying CNR, which has a 10-year average yield of 1.60%, which likely places it near the bottom of your "Yield Difference" worksheet.

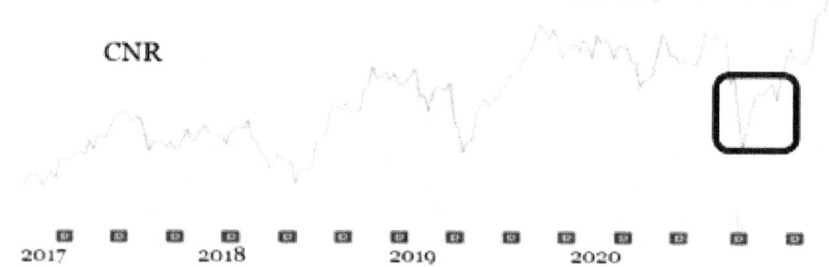

Looking at the chart above, in December 2018, the market dropped suddenly, but quickly recovered. If you were unable to buy CNR at that time, you will notice that the price of CNR rose steadily then levelled off, with a quick one-month dip March 2019.

From March 2019 to March 2020, the price of CNR averaged about $118.09. If you had set your "price and yield" range for CNR during this period, it's likely you would have set the low price close to $113.00, a 4% drop in price.

There was an unexpected price drop in February 2020 when CNR hit $113.79 and then dropped further in March 2020 to a low of $99.33. CNR rose quickly, but there was an opportunity during April and May 2020, a

INCOME INVESTING EXPLAINED

two-month period, when one

CNR	Price	Div	Yield	10-Yr Ave Yld	Yield Diff
FEB 2\20	$125.28	$2.15	1.72%	1.62%	0.10%
MAR 15\20	$99.33	$2.15	2.17%	1.62%	0.55%
MAY 10\20	$110.00	$2.30	2.09%	1.62%	0.47%

could have bought CNR for around $107.00 to $111.00.

In the chart above, it shows that one could have bought CNR at a price well below its high of $125.28 in February 2020. The yield difference shown for March and May 2020 may not seem like much, but CNR has had a 10-year dividend growth rate of about 260% and the price of CNR has followed that dividend growth (see chart below). I think, for a normally expensive stock, this would have been a good opportunity to

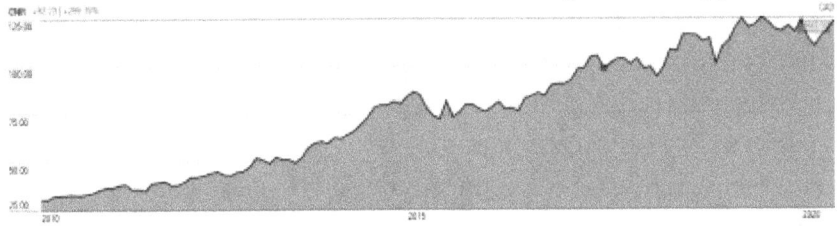

buy CNR at a reasonable price.

It is during market corrections that you should take advantage of the opportunity to buy those stocks which were always at the bottom of your "Yield Difference" worksheet. Even if you can get a higher yield from the stocks you already own, or with ones that have a much higher yield difference, I suggest you consider buying those previously expensive stocks.

You don't need to buy at the stock market bottom, just at a much better price than you can normally buy them at. I really want to take this opportunity to stress a point that is often lost in the decision-making process of when to buy:

Expensive stocks tend to be at the bottom of your "Yield Difference" list, but you'll gain much more over the next 10 or more years acquiring those stocks at a reasonable price then you will from most of the other stocks on your list bought at a great price. The best stocks are normally expensive for a good reason!

How long will you be investing?

This section is a little philosophical. Looking ahead can be difficult. No one knows how long we'll live or if we'll maintain our health. But we'd all like to live as long as possible and believe we'll live to a ripe old age. So, when you are looking to buy stocks, consider just how long you might be holding them for:

- If you are 35, you could have 30 years of potential growth and possibly another 30 years of retirement, or a total of 60 years.
- If you are 45, you could have 20 years of potential growth and possibly 30 years of retirement, or a total of 50 years.
- If you are 55, you could have 10 years of potential growth and another 30 years of retirement, or a total of 40 years.

You can see that there are a lot of years available to a lot of people to accumulate wealth, and at least 25 to 30 years of retirement to be funded. So why not invest in the best Income growth stocks which offer the greatest chance of success? Security in retirement is a very pressing issue, and one we all seek. One of the main reasons for writing my books is to help people attain that security. I don't offer a magic wand, but a realistic and reasonable strategy. It has worked for me, there is no reason it won't work for you.

If you're trying to guess the bottom, don't!

When the market suffers a crash or an extended drop, it's impossible to determine when the lowest point will occur. When the market has a sudden drop, as it did during the Covid-19 crisis of March 2020, we saw a real drop in prices of about 35%, then a quick recovery, but prices were still 15% to 20% below the February high. At the time of writing this book, it is still anyone's guess if the market will go lower, trade within a narrow range or continue recovering.

The rectangular area below shows the TSX from February 20th to April 30th, 2020. The lowest drop, during this period, was March 23rd. If one had been able to buy stocks from March 11th to April 7th, indicated by the inner circled section, they would

TSX Index Chart

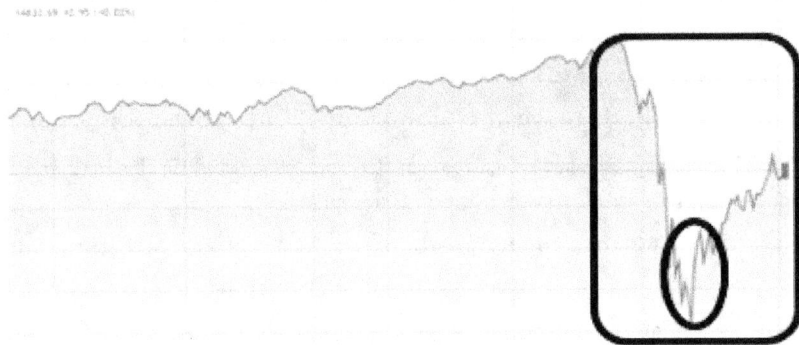

have bought almost any stock at an exceptionally low price.

Often, one will not be able to buy during the initial drop in price, because the market recovers too quickly, or possibly because the markets halt all trading. Even after the price has recovered a bit, people are often hesitant to buy, caught up instead with thinking the market will drop again. This is a mistake, in my opinion. Investors are always hesitant to buy when the price drops suddenly, worried it might drop even further. This is where panic and greed set in. Instead of realizing the rare advantage of a 15% to 20% price drop, one becomes paralyzed as you worry that the price may go even lower, or you fret about the drop in the value of your stocks.

It seems that people forget that when the market is rising, a 1% or 2% price drop looks like a real bargain. At the same time a half of a percent yield increase is welcomed. Why anyone would hesitate to buy those quality stocks you've already identified, when the market is down 15% or more and the yield increase may be 1% or more, is a wonder to me.

Every 1% increase in your initial yield purchases will normally take three years of normal dividend increases to obtain the same yield increase.

The following example explains this in more detail. The chart below shows a dividend growth of 7% each year:

Initial Yield	Dividend growth @ 7% each year			
	Year 1	Year 2	Year 3	Year 4
3.50%	3.75%	4.01%	4.29%	4.59%
4.00%	4.28%	4.58%	4.90%	5.24%
4.25%	4.55%	4.87%	5.21%	5.57%
4.50%	4.82%	5.15%	5.51%	5.90%
4.75%	5.08%	5.44%	5.82%	6.23%
5.00%	5.35%	5.72%	6.13%	6.55%

Think about that. Getting 1% higher yield on a purchase is like waiting three years to obtain the same yield at normal dividend increases. But don't look for higher yielding stocks, rather look for the opportunity to buy your quality stocks when the stock market has a correction.

We can't know in advance when or if there will be a market correction, but when they do happen, you will have lots of opportunity to find stocks with more than reasonable yields.

If prices drop again after you buy, don't feel bad. The market just as easily could have gone up. If you were able to buy one of your quality stocks with a 1/2% or higher than its previous yield you should be satisfied. Look at it this way, you bought a stock which offered a reasonable yield, you've increased your portfolio income, and hopefully you achieved the objective of lowering the yield on your total investments.

Who determines market movement?

Individual investors might know that market movement is a result of supply and demand, but do they really know what that means. Stock prices change every day, moving up if more people want to buy a stock (causing a demand), or moving down if more people wish to sell (increasing supply). But individuals play just a small part in market behaviour. What most don't realize is that we, individual investors, don't have much effect on the market at all. It is really the "institutional investor" that plays the biggest role. Institutional investors are the mutual funds, ETFs, hedge funds and even some of the pension fund organizations. They buy and sell at much higher volumes, and regularly, to rebalance or shift their investments, seeking growth opportunities, much more so than individual investors. Institutional investors account for at least 70% of stock trading. What they do, and when, is really what causes the price of shares to move up and down.

Economic, political, and even company performance does play an important role, but more often it is how the institutional investors interrupt those events, and how they react to them, that cause price movement.

If you invest for price growth, a good way to look at the individual investor's relationship is:

It's like being part of a team, but whether you play or not, your input has little or no effect on the outcome of the game.

You win or lose if the team (the market) wins or loses, but mostly you're just along for the ride. In other words, your future growth is dependent upon the market growing, and there is no payment for just participating!

That's why I suggest you change the way you play the investment game, start being in control, rather than giving that control away.

As an individual investor, we can't change the fact that we have no control over market movements, but we can change how we play the "game". We can be more selective as to which stocks we buy. We can try to stick with stocks which will pay you income and grow the income they pay, whether the market is moving up or down. So now, as well as getting paid for the team's winning record (the value of our stocks going up), we'll also receive a growing income whether the team wins or loses. You will get paid for just participating! You won't have to worry if and when others might cause the value of your holdings to fluctuate. Your payments for playing the investment "game" won't be at the whim of market behaviour, where you have no control, and with institutional investors who don't have your best interests at heart. Stop playing the guessing game, there's no reason you have to lose when you didn't even ask to play!

The even tougher decision, when to sell

Everyone would like to sell their stocks when prices are up, and you make a large profit. It's the primary reason most people buy stocks. What I see happening is that when the market is booming, most people have difficulty convincing themselves that the market won't just continue to rise. So, they hold on, hedging their bets. Often, I find investors getting hooked on the thrill of rising prices and do not think of the risk they're taking. Others will sell during up markets, taking profits, then seek new stocks to buy at lower prices. This is the guessing game, hoping that your sales make a profit and that you'll be able to find another winner to buy low and sell later for more profit. This has always been easier said than done. And this is also why I do not subscribe to this way of investing.

For Income investors, selling should be a rare thing, no matter what the market is doing. This is the reason you spend so much time searching, evaluating and screening out stocks to arrive at your "List of Stocks to Consider". When you do buy, your intention should be to hold them for the income and the continued income growth you expect.

Other than REALLY needing the money, there are only a few occasions that one should consider selling part or all of your holdings of a particular stock. I've made this point several times in my earlier books: *As long as your company stocks continue to pay their dividend as expected, and they grow the dividend at a reasonable rate (5% or higher each year), you should never sell the stock.*

Ok, I will admit there are times when you might be better off selling. For an Income investor the reasons to consider selling might be:

1. If you hold a stock which you bought because it offered a higher initial yield (6% or above), but a lower dividend growth rate (less than 3% per year).
2. One of your stocks stopped raising its dividend by at least 3% and you are concerned that the dividend growth may remain low or even stop increasing.
3. The yield of a stock rises above 7% and you feel the company may be

in financial difficulty and might need to cut their dividend.

Should any of the above conditions apply to one or more of the stocks you own, you might wish to consider selling part or all of the holdings of a company. The best time to consider selling is when markets are booming, as they did from March 2009 thru February 2020, as shown in the chart below. During bull markets you will have lots of time and opportunity to consider selling.

However, many investors will hesitate or not consider selling when the markets are rising, because:

- The stock is not worth what you originally paid for it.

- You might believe the price will rise and you will regain the loss.

- You may be lulled into a false security because the market is rising.

- You might not have kept on top of your stocks and don't realize you are holding a stock which you should consider selling.

Taking all of this into consideration, I think we can determine when one should consider selling:

- If the current yield of a "lower-quality" stock rises above 7%. This is often the first sign of "trouble", and if it occurs you should seriously look for a chance to sell.

- If you've seen one of your stocks slowly "slump", especially if that "slumping" is indicated by a lack of an increased dividend as expected, and if dividend growth gradually slows.

- If one of your quality dividend growth stocks year-to-year dividend increase falls below the 3% minimum over the previous year.

	2010	2011	2012	2013	2014	2015	2016	2017	2018	2019	Gth/Yld Ave
Dividend	1.21	1.46	1.59	1.88	1.92	1.96	2.00	2.04	2.08	2.12	75.21%
% Chg		20.66%	8.90%	18.24%	2.13%	2.08%	2.04%	2.00%	1.96%	1.92%	

As soon as the dividend stops growing at a reasonable rate, start thinking about the possibility of selling, but don't take the decision to sell lightly. I have provided an example below for you to consider. Look at the year-to-year dividend growth rates each year and how they dropped and stayed down from 2014. Yes, the dividend continued to increase each year, but at an extremely low rate.

1. After the first year, the dividend dropped below 3%. This should be an indication to start looking for an explanation.
2. By the second year of less than 3% dividend growth, you should be assessing the reasons you might wish to continue to hold the stock or sell.
    - Is the company acknowledging any issues and makes you believe they will be able to recover quickly?
    - Have you owned the stock for a long time and your yield on the investment is generating a high yield (above 7%)?
    - Do you feel that the company will continue to have positive earnings and be able to maintain the low growth rate, even possibly increase it later?
    - If you do sell, do you have a replacement which will provide a reasonable return and better growth prospects?

Here is the same stock, showing 20 years of year-to-year

	2000	2001	2002	2003	2004	2005	2006	2007	2008	2009
Div % Chg	20.00%	14.74%	7.95%	31.34%	11.67%	15.38%	44.44%	20.00%	7.14%	16.67%

	2010	2011	2012	2013	2014	2015	2016	2017	2018	2019
Div % Chg	11.01%	20.66%	8.90%	18.24%	2.13%	2.08%	2.04%	2.00%	1.96%	1.92%

dividend percentage changes:

As you can see, had you owned this stock from 2000 to 2013, you would have seen an average year-to-year dividend growth of 17.72%. Of course, with this performance, you'd be really hesitant to consider selling this stock, in fact I'd probably never consider selling at that time. But by 2015, and definitely by 2016, you should now be looking at the reasons why you should <u>not</u> be selling. This situation emphasizes why you should never get complacent. This stock has probably reached its limit for earnings growth, and is now finding it difficult to expand and is just maintaining its earnings at a level rate.

You should monitor all the stocks you own, be aware of their dividend growth history and be mentally prepared to make the decision to sell if any of the companies show signs of lowering their dividend growth rate. Look for signs that economic factors may affect their performance.

If you made the decision to hold a stock, don't panic if the market does drop suddenly. Or if you had planned to sell, but are caught off guard and the market experiences a correction, be prepared to hold until the market recovers. It may take months or even years, but the market has demonstrated that it always recovers from a correction or crisis, sometimes even coming back stronger than ever.

There is benefit to sitting back and waiting for the next

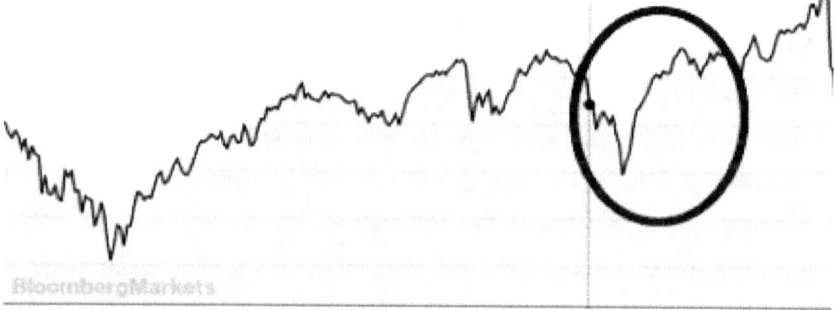

INCOME INVESTING EXPLAINED

recovery, as shown in the chart below:

Let's look at a more recent example of a good stock which has suffered a reversal. Inter Pipelines Ltd. is a good example to use to illustrate this point. From 2010 to 2015, the dividend growth was good.

IPL	2010	2011	2012	2013	2014	2015	2016	2017	2018	2019	Gth/Yld Ave
Dividend	0.91	0.97	1.05	1.18	1.32	1.49	1.57	1.63	1.69	1.71	87.91%
% Chg		6.59%	8.25%	12.38%	11.86%	12.88%	5.37%	3.82%	3.68%	1.18%	

But look at the drop in the dividend growth beginning in 2016. Being a smaller pipeline company, it did not have the resources to withstand the drop in oil prices, nor the cash reserves of the larger pipelines. The industry has been embattled as of late and the price of its shares had already dropped even before the Covid-19 crisis. Also, its dividend yield had exceeded 7% for several years, reaching 8% in 2018.

From October 2019 to February 2020, the share price remained stable at around $21.00 (shown in the chart below), and the dividend yield was at least 8.1%. One should have expected the dividend yield could not remain above 8% for an extended period without a cut.

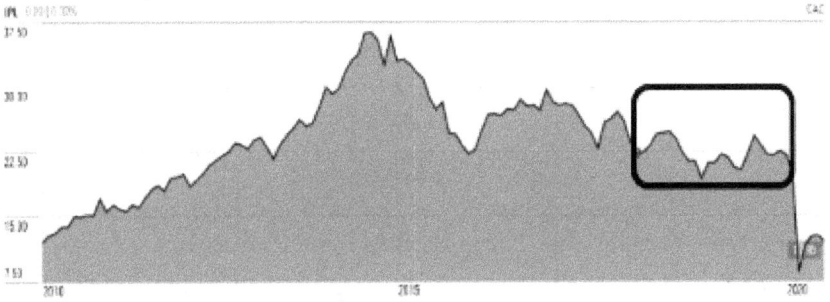

To me, the signs were there, and no one should have been surprised when Inter Pipelines cut their dividend by 72% in April 2020.

Best time to sell your "losers"?

There will be times when you will have made a mistake. You may have taken a chance on a higher yielding stock or you might have bought a stock that did well for years, but then the dividend gets cut and there's no recovery in sight. We've all bought a few of those. You think you're doing the right thing by holding on to the stock, believing it will recover, but sometimes it doesn't.

At times like these, the best thing to do is cut your losses. Yes, you'll take a loss, but the question is how big of a loss? It might not be that bad of a stock, but you have come to realize that it's not really a quality dividend growth stock. But when do you make the decision to sell?

The easiest decision is made when you hear these three words: **"All Time High"**. Maybe you don't think you'll hear those words that often. Well, actually you will, especially in a bull

market, as we experienced after the 2008 financial crisis.

The first circle on the chart above is the peak of the TSX before the 2008 financial crisis. Each circle after that shows when the TSX hit an all-time high, all the way until the Covid-19 health crisis of 2020.

In fact, there were seven "All Time Highs" before the Covid-19 crisis brought the market down again. Here are the dates of each all-time-high and the length of time until the next high:

1. May 2008, high before financial crisis
2. Apr 2014, 6 years after May 2008
3. June 2017, 3 years from 2014
4. Nov. 2017, 11 months from June 2017

INCOME INVESTING EXPLAINED

5. Aug. 2018 9 months from Nov 2017
6. Sep. 2019, 11 months from Aug 2018
7. Feb. 2020, 5 months from Sep 2019

Because of these continuous market highs, even if you had suffered a loss due to the financial crisis, and you are still experiencing a loss, you would have had lots of opportunity to sell, especially from November 2017 to February 2020.

If you hold a "loser" and the market is growing, then look for a chance to sell and reinvest the funds in a quality dividend growth stock which will offer you the chance to recoup your losses and grow your income. Ask yourself if a 10% or higher loss might not be worth absorbing, if you can invest those funds in a stock which has provided 8% to 10% growth for the past few years and you expect the growth to continue.

Remember that when I refer to "losers" we are talking about long-time under-performing stocks, not necessarily one of your quality holdings which might have suffered a reversal, a debt issue or one that just slowed its dividend growth rate.

Once you've decided you want to get rid of an under-performing stock, set a "selling range" and monitor the market, looking for a period where you feel the market is rising and will likely hit one of the "All-Time Highs". If the market does reach an acceptable level, don't second guess yourself, take your loss or sell when you've hit your sell range and move on.

Since I love to give examples to illustrate my points, let's assume you talked yourself into buying Pizza Pizza Royalty Corp (PZA) in 2013, because, who doesn't love pizza? The price chart from 2013 thru 2018 looks reasonable. The initial yield of PZA in 2013 was 5.89% and it paid a monthly

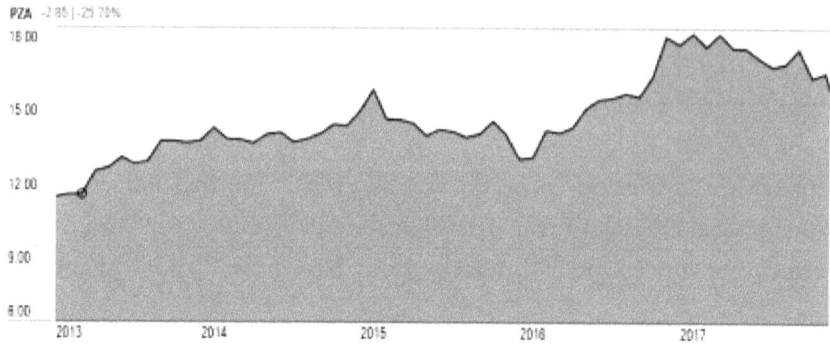

dividend.

Pizza Pizza paid a nice yield, but had little dividend growth after 2013 and the yield began rising after 2016.

PZA	2010	2011	2012	2013	2014	2015	2016	2017	2018	2019	10 Yr Gth%
Dividend	0.94	0.70	0.72	0.77	0.80	0.82	0.85	0.85	0.85	0.85	-8.97%
Div Gth Yr		-25.64%	2.73%	8.25%	3.88%	1.62%	3.67%	0.59%	0.00%	0.00%	

If you were monitoring the stock and applying reasonable sell guidelines, you should have been alerted that the dividend was faltering after 2014. Had you been watching the dividend growth, you might have considered selling any time after 2016, but if you waited until mid-2018, look what happened.

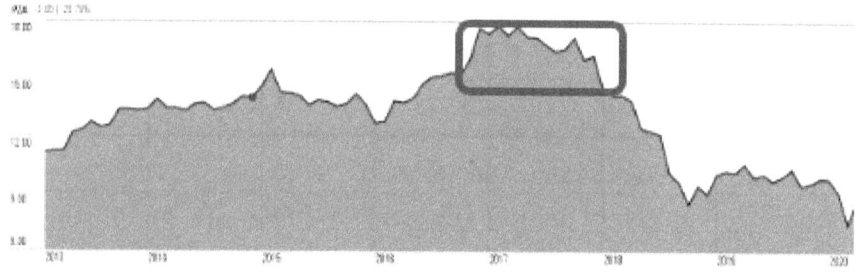

By 2018 the dividend yield had risen to 9.52%, a clear sign that the dividend is unsafe, and sure enough, it was cut in 2020. What might have seemed a good idea at one time, ended up getting "burnt to a crisp".

I think this is a valuable lesson that all investors should learn. Always monitor your stocks, and especially watch any stock which may be of lesser quality. Markers to look for are the following:

1. If the dividend yield is 3% higher than the dividend paid by other companies in the same sector.
2. The dividend is 3% higher than its 10-year average dividend yield.

3. The dividend growth has fallen below 3% each year.
4. The dividend yield is 7% or higher.
5. Is there any troublesome news about the industry which causes concern and may affect the stock you own?
6. If the company announces that the dividend will not be increased, be very wary.

However, if any of these concerns should present themselves, don't immediately react by selling. Consider the following:

1. Take the time to review the stock and calculate how much of a capital loss you might take, or what the capital gain will be.
2. Ask yourself if you might be better off if the funds were invested in another stock, even if you have to sell at a loss.
3. If you feel you might be better off selling, set the sell price or range.
4. If the sell price is reached, don't hesitate, even if the market is booming.
5. If you've made a decision to sell a stock, but the market drops, rather than rising, you may still have to take a loss and invest your funds elsewhere.

There is no right answer when it comes to shedding losing stocks. It is not something an Income investor should need to do often, but it cannot be ruled out as a possibility either. Avoiding "losers" is one of the reasons I've stressed the importance of trying to identify the best stocks you can for your "List of Stocks to Consider". We still may make a mistake, but likely they will not be classified as "losers", rather they may still be a good company but have been affected by economic or unforeseen factors. Enbridge is an example of a company that fits this bill, as they've suffered the same economic problems as Inter Pipelines. But even though there is a higher debt issue, Enbridge continues to maintain its position as a good dividend growth stock.

In summary, look to sell those stocks which you feel have not performed as well as expected, especially when the market is rising. You may even be better off taking a capital loss, if you can reinvest the funds in a better-quality stock at a reasonable price.

If you bought a lower quality stock, possibly for its higher yield, it's unlikely it will perform well, even when markets are rising. If the market makes a correction, it is the lower quality stocks which will likely cut their dividend and take the longest to recover.

This is why I use the word "reasonable" so often. Look for those quality stocks which offer a reasonable yield, reasonable growth and reasonable returns.

Should you sell a long-time good stock that cuts the dividend?

This is a tough question to answer, and one that is more relevant now than ever. The best I can say is that it depends upon the reason for the dividend cut, economic factors and how quickly one thinks the company might be able to recover.

To help us get a better understanding of this conundrum, let's look at the following examples:

TransCanada Pipeline: In 1999 TransCanada Pipelines Ltd., Canada's biggest natural gas pipeline operator, sold assets and cut its dividend by a third, from $1.12 to 0.80, to cut costs and reduce debt.

TransCanada's stock price did drop as well, but it appears that investors believed that reducing their debt should be a priority and the dividend cut was justified. The chart below shows that not only did the stock price recover quickly, but the company reinstated dividend increases within a year. Since this episode, TRP could be considered one of the most stable dividend-growth stocks available.

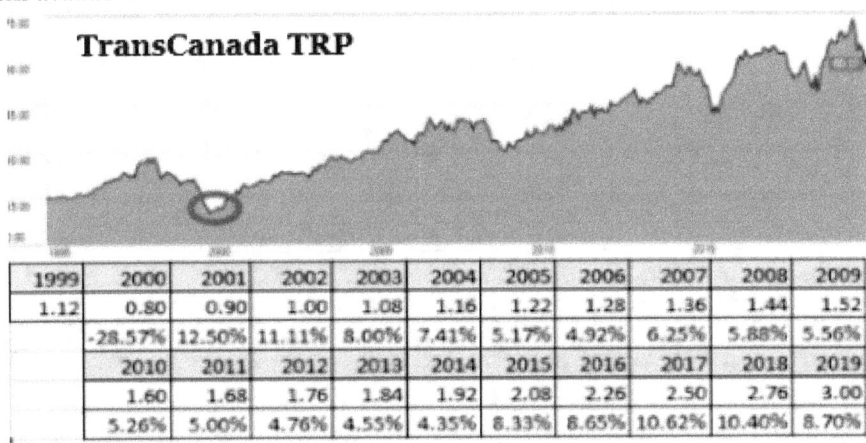

1999	2000	2001	2002	2003	2004	2005	2006	2007	2008	2009
1.12	0.80	0.90	1.00	1.08	1.16	1.22	1.28	1.36	1.44	1.52
	-28.57%	12.50%	11.11%	8.00%	7.41%	5.17%	4.92%	6.25%	5.88%	5.56%
	2010	2011	2012	2013	2014	2015	2016	2017	2018	2019
	1.60	1.68	1.76	1.84	1.92	2.08	2.26	2.50	2.76	3.00
	5.26%	5.00%	4.76%	4.55%	4.35%	8.33%	8.65%	10.62%	10.40%	8.70%

Telus: In 2001, Telus Corp. slashed its quarterly dividend by more than half, stating the widely expected move would free up cash to push its wireless and Internet strategies and drive its telecommunications growth.

In 2001, Telus was expanding from a provincial to a national telecommunications provider. The decision to reduce the dividend was accepted and once the company established its position the dividend increases were reinstated and have continued to increase to date. It also has had a stellar record of increasing its dividend ever since. The chart below shows when Telus cut their dividend and the gains since then.

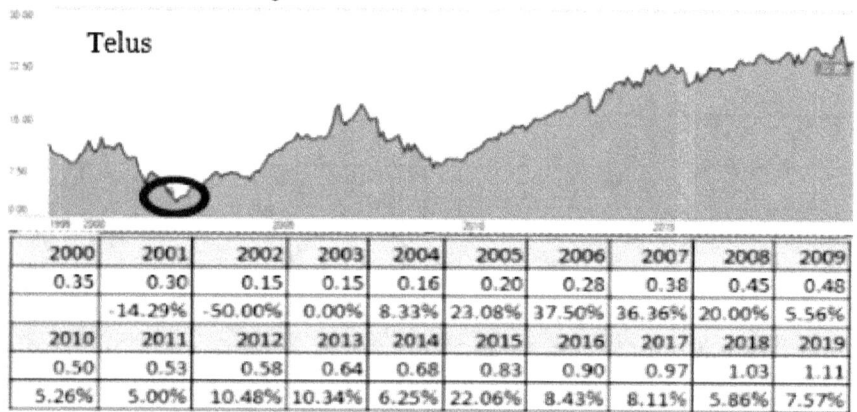

2000	2001	2002	2003	2004	2005	2006	2007	2008	2009
0.35	0.30	0.15	0.15	0.16	0.20	0.28	0.38	0.45	0.48
	-14.29%	-50.00%	0.00%	8.33%	23.08%	37.50%	36.36%	20.00%	5.56%
2010	2011	2012	2013	2014	2015	2016	2017	2018	2019
0.50	0.53	0.58	0.64	0.68	0.83	0.90	0.97	1.03	1.11
5.26%	5.00%	10.48%	10.34%	6.25%	22.06%	8.43%	8.11%	5.86%	7.57%

Manulife: In 2009 during the financial crisis, the price of Manulife shares fell nearly 50 per cent. When Manulife declared a dividend cut (circled area on the chart below), due to debt issues and low interest rates, the share price dropped almost 15% in a single day.

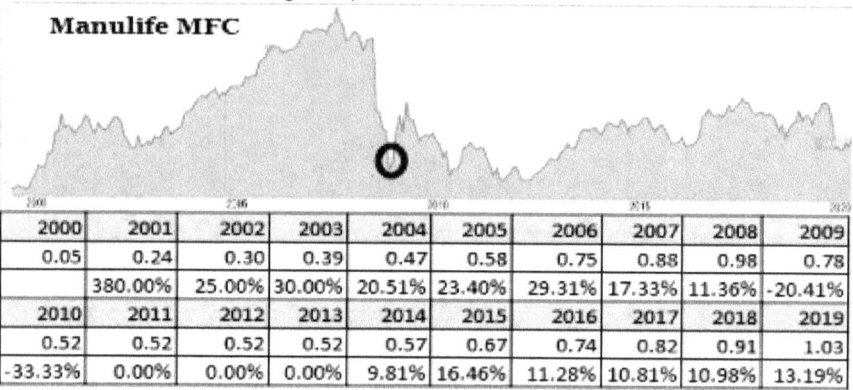

2000	2001	2002	2003	2004	2005	2006	2007	2008	2009
0.05	0.24	0.30	0.39	0.47	0.58	0.75	0.88	0.98	0.78
	380.00%	25.00%	30.00%	20.51%	23.40%	29.31%	17.33%	11.36%	-20.41%
2010	2011	2012	2013	2014	2015	2016	2017	2018	2019
0.52	0.52	0.52	0.52	0.57	0.67	0.74	0.82	0.91	1.03
-33.33%	0.00%	0.00%	0.00%	9.81%	16.46%	11.28%	10.81%	10.98%	13.19%

Manulife needed to cut their dividend in 2009, not just because of the financial crisis, but because of an undisclosed debt the company had incurred. To compound their problems, interest rates dropped to almost zero. The chart above shows how it took five years before the company was again in a position to begin raising their dividend. Since 2015, the dividend growth rate has been 12% per year, but its share price has not recovered from the 2008 high.

Summary: All three companies, TransCanada (now T C Energy), Telus and Manulife were considered quality dividend growth stocks before they cut their dividend.

The difference seems to be that TransCanada and Telus acknowledged the reasons for the cut and most investors believed the cut was necessary or justified.

The debt of Manulife came as a surprise to investors and coupled with economic factors, investors were less inclined to believe the company would recover quickly. It took six years before the company began increasing their dividend, and the share price still has not recovered.

Let me add that if you had a 20-year investment timeline you might wish to add to Manulife, rather than sell. Manulife is still the largest insurance company in Canada and the price of its shares has remained low. It took 10 years for the dividend to recover and by adding to your shares, you would have bought them at a depressed price. The dividend growth for the past six years has been above average.

There are occasions that selling a stock may be necessary, and a dividend cut is definitely a red flag. Though it is difficult to predict what a company will do, if you have strong suspicions of a pending cut, it may be wise to consider selling.

However, for the quality dividend growth companies that we prize, I might consider holding on, or even buying more shares when the cut occurs, provided the company is up-front with the reasons for the cut and prospects look good for the company going forward. Dividend cuts will affect your income, but they may not be a death blow when you are holding nothing but quality company stocks.

Income investors succeed because of their due diligence, patience, and measured reactions. Often investors are trapped watching the market and media, and not making informed decisions but simply reacting to forces beyond their control. Income investing offers an alternative. Stay vigilant, know the companies you own and be prepared.

How can we avoid dividend cuts?

I mentioned earlier that no company, not even a strong company with a long history of dividend growth, is immune to a dividend cut. There is no crystal ball, we don't really know when a company will cut their dividend, but there are signs to look for and things you can do to lessen the chance of suffering a dividend cut.

1. Avoid buying lower-quality stocks whose initial dividend yield is 6% or higher. To me, this is a clear signal that the dividend is not safe, even if they've paid a dividend for years and raised their dividend periodically. Some REITs and Income Trusts offer attractive yields, but usually their dividend growth rate is low. If you bought such a stock offering a yield of 6%, and it rises to 7% or higher, this should be your "Canary in a Coal Mine".

1. Be on the look-out if the year-to-year dividend growth rate percentage falls below 3%. Dividends are paid from company earnings, and if a company has a long history of raising the dividend by at least 5% each year, and suddenly it drops below 3%, take notice. Likely, the earnings have dropped, which may be a sign of other issues you are not aware of.

1. Be wary if the current dividend yield of a quality stock rises 3% above its 10-year average dividend yield. Many quality companies have had periods where their current yields were above 3% over their 10-year average and have not had to cut their dividend.

The 3% difference is not a red flag, but it's certainly a yellow flag. Use this as a sign that you should be searching for the cause of the increase in the yield.

- Has the company acknowledged, or explained the cause?

- Can the increase be explained by current events which might not affect the company's earnings?

- Has the company missed their quarterly earnings estimate?

If a company falls into any of the above three categories, you should be looking at the company's payout ratio as well as its free cash-flow history. The payout ratio is your indicator that sales or earnings have fallen, and the company must pay out a higher percentage of their earnings to meet its dividend obligation. If the company has a high payout ratio, but good free cash-flow, then it may be in a position to continue paying the dividend without a cut.

What is a reasonable Payout Ratio?

Definition: *"A lower **payout ratio** indicates that a **company** is retaining more of its earnings to fuel its growth, whereas a higher **payout ratio** indicates that a **company** is sharing more of its earnings with stockholders. A **payout ratio** of more than 100% means that a **company's** dividend payments are exceeding its net income"*

Usually the lower the payout ratio the better, especially if the company continues to raise the dividend. But what is considered high, or too high? It depends upon the company, the sector the company is in and current market and/or economic conditions. Some companies suddenly find themselves with lower earnings because of factors out of their control, others might find themselves with higher debt or an expansion which did not generate expected earnings. All of these things can affect the payout ratio. However, there are steps companies can take to resolve or address the issues. How quickly these steps will correct or lower the payout ratio will vary.

Having said the above, we can categorize and suggest reasonable payout ratios for various sectors:

Consumer 40% to 65%
Energy 60% to 75%
Financials 40% to 60%
Telecom 65% to 75%

Utilities 65% to 75%

REITs 85% to 95%

What makes REITs and Income trusts attractive is that many provide higher yields and monthly distributions. Monthly distributions can really contribute to compounding and many have earned some nice income from them. The problem is that they are required to distribute most of their earnings (85% to 95%) and should their earnings drop, so will the distribution. Too risky in my opinion.

After saying this, does that mean any payout ratio above 75% is a concern? Not really, as I mentioned before, there are a number of reasons why a company payout ratio may rise above a reasonable ratio, so the dividend will probably be safe. There are companies which have free cash flows which will allow the company to continue to meet their dividend commitments and continue raising the dividend even though the payout ratio is high.

Remember that payout ratios are based on previous earnings and one must look at more than just how the company has performed, but also at what the future prospects are for the company. Does it appear that company earnings will remain low? Are the lower earnings a result of poor management decisions or economic factors which could not have been predicted, such as the Covid-19 crisis? Do you see the company continuing to maintain a strong position and grow?

Should the payout ratio be close to or above 100% for a company, then one should be hesitant to buy more shares unless you seriously look at their future prospects or their financial strength and come away satisfied. How strong is the company's balance sheet? If there is high debt, is it reasonable to expect that the company can handle it and eventually reduce the debt? Some of these questions may be difficult to answer, and therefore, you should just play it safe and not buy shares when the payout ratio is high.

As a side note, companies with payout ratios of 25% and lower, will likely be "low yield, high growth" stocks, such as MRU and ATD.B. These are usually the expensive stocks on your list. Personally, I like to see the payout ratio stable between 40% to 70%. That tells me the company is committed to allocating a good portion of their earning to their shareholders, but still holding sufficient funds in reserve for other needs.

There is always a chance that even the highest-rated dividend growth stock may cut their dividend. It has happened in the past, and even today, with the health crisis of 2020, solid companies are dealing with unprecedented economic turmoil.

Several companies have cut their dividend during the Covid-19 crisis, mainly energy stocks, including some solid companies like Suncor, which had raised its dividend 17 consecutive years prior to the cut. Oil prices have been dropping for some time and many energy companies were already suffering, but Suncor seemed to be weathering the storm. In fact, it raised its dividend in January 2020, but then had to cut it during the Covid-19 crisis a short time later. In hindsight, as soon as oil prices started dropping and trouble in the industry was widely discussed, you could have taken the opportunity to divest yourself of these stocks as a precaution. I don't like, nor recommend knee-jerk responses, but the energy sector became particularly vulnerable very quickly. I do consider energy stocks as cyclical and have recommended they not be considered among your quality dividend growth stocks, even if their dividend growth numbers are positive.

The main thing I want you to take away from this section is that by concentrating on the highest quality dividend growth stocks, with a reasonable payout ratio, you can lessen the risk of dividend cuts. But you must also couple this with a commitment to maintaining vigilance for the warning signs.

Do companies have to raise their dividend every year?

Regular and predictable dividend increases are what every dividend growth investor wants and hopes for. But is it mandatory that you only own company stocks which have raised their dividend each and every year? Not necessarily.

Although I make dividend increases a part of my evaluation criteria, there are stocks that can be exceptions to this rule. If you take a look at the following example, you will see that the dividend of this particular bank stock remained at 0.70 cents

STOCK PURCHASES				DIVIDEND REINVESTMENT				
Date	Price	Shares	Cost	Date	Price	Shares	Div Rec'd	Div
Oct 15\07	55.00	1.0000	55.00				0.00	
Nov 30\07	58.32	171.4678	10000.00	Nov 30\07	58.3159	0.0120	0.70	0.70
Jan 31\08	56.56	88.4017	5000.00	Feb 29\08	53.9800	3.383105	182.62	0.70
Sep 30\08	46.40	107.7586	5000.00	May 0\08	48.3300	3.827643	184.99	0.70
May 29\09	47.82	209.1175	10000.00	Aug 29\08	44.9300	4.176719	187.66	0.70
Nov 30\09	53.11	47.07211	2500.00	Nov 28\08	34.2400	7.769276	266.02	0.70
Apr 29\11	62.67	31.9132	2000.00	Feb 27\09	25.4400	10.6706	271.46	0.70
			0.00	May 29\09	41.4100	6.735813	278.93	0.70
			0.00	Aug 31\09	51.2600	8.388997	430.02	0.70
			0.00	Nov 30\09	52.0500	8.37464	435.90	0.70
			0.00	Feb 27\10	53.9300	8.802336	474.71	0.70
			0.00	May 29\10	59.3200	8.106372	480.87	0.70
			0.00	Aug 31\10	55.5600	8.757199	486.55	0.70
			0.00	Nov 30\10	60.2200	8.181335	492.68	0.70
			0.00	Feb 27\11	61.2600	8.135815	498.40	0.70
			0.00	May 29\11	61.7900	8.510725	525.88	0.70
			0.00	Aug 31\11	59.8300	8.898546	532.40	0.70
			0.00	Nov 30\11	56.2200	9.580754	538.63	0.70
			0.00	Feb 27\12	57.0700	9.555633	545.34	0.70
			0.00	May 29\12	53.5100	10.31639	552.03	0.70
			0.00	Aug 31\12	56.6100	9.878997	559.25	0.70
			0.00	Nov 28\12	59.2200	9.833502	582.34	0.72

from November 2007 thru to August 2012:

The chart shows that the income ("Div Rec'd" column) from this investment grew each quarter, even though the dividend had not increased.

This example is a Canadian bank stock. The initial investment was made before the financial crisis, meaning that the price of the stock was on the high side and most of the shares were bought before the financial crisis and prices dropped. Even though this bank did not raise its dividend for four and a half years and additional funds were not added after April 2011, the income from the investment continued to increase each and every quarter.

I would like you to pay attention to the fractions of shares added each quarter. Fractions of shares do make a difference, they will increase the number of shares you own, the income you earn and you benefit from the compounding effect the longer you own the stock. Fractions of shares are especially important for those investors that can only afford to invest small amounts, those who don't add funds often, and retired investors. For retired investors who can no longer

INCOME INVESTING EXPLAINED

add funds to an RRSP or RRIF, any money left after buying full shares will

Date	Price	Shares	Div Rec'd	Div
Nov 28\12	59.2200	9.833502	582.34	0.72
Feb 27\13	63.2500	9.318893	589.42	0.72
May 29\13	62.9100	9.739151	612.69	0.74
Aug 31\13	65.5537	9.456217	619.89	0.74
Nov 30\13	74.0411	8.466784	626.89	0.74
Feb 27\14	72.9347	8.915784	650.27	0.76
May 29\14	76.4500	8.594506	657.05	0.76
Aug 31\14	80.7300	8.436021	681.04	0.78
Nov 30\14	83.3300	8.25177	687.62	0.78
Feb 27\15	77.6840	9.163406	711.85	0.80
May 29\15	78.0973	9.208769	719.18	0.80
Aug 31\15	70.4934	10.56425	744.71	0.82
Nov 30\15	76.6787	9.825154	753.38	0.82
Feb 27\16	74.2718	10.50197	780.00	0.84
May 29\16	83.0000	9.503976	788.83	0.84
Aug 31\16	85.5600	9.534596	815.78	0.86
Nov 30\16	86.9100	9.480842	823.98	0.86
Feb 27\17	98.6500	8.631424	851.49	0.88
May 29\17	92.9000	9.247363	859.08	0.88
Aug 31\17	92.0737	9.632827	886.93	0.90
Nov 30\17	99.3450	9.015049	895.60	0.90
Feb 27\18	99.0728	9.425796	933.84	0.93
May 29\18	101.5353	9.283471	942.60	0.93
Aug 31\18	106.3281	9.234812	981.92	0.96
Nov 30\18	97.6478	10.14657	990.79	0.96
Feb 27\19	98.9170	10.53631	1042.22	1.00
May 29\19	103.3180	10.18942	1052.75	1.00
Aug 31\19	93.1183	11.75741	1094.83	1.03
Nov 30\19	101.3495	10.92201	1106.94	1.03

just sit in the account unused or becomes "dead money".

A long history of dividend increases is important as part of your initial evaluation and selection process, but after you've bought a stock, don't feel you must sell if the company does not raise their dividend each and every year thereafter. Take the time to determine why a company, which has a long history of raising their dividend, suddenly holds off on increasing the dividend.

I also wanted to show with this example that a lack of dividend increases is not a sign of failure. Canadian banks were restricted from raising their dividend during the financial crisis of 2008 by the Canadian government, until their cash reserves increased. I considered this a circumstance that was necessary, actually a smart move, which confirmed my faith in the security and stability of banks as quality dividend stocks. The prices of the bank stocks plummeted, as did all stocks during the financial crisis, but was not compounded because they also had stopped raising their dividends. The wise investor should have seen the lower prices as buying opportunities.

I have used the term "dividend growth" in this and my other books, but really, I mean "income growth". Dividend increases play a big part in generating a growing income from your investments, but not exclusively, as the example above demonstrates.

Do stock splits make a difference?

Corporations split their shares for many reasons, but mainly to make the shares more attractive to buy, as the price of buying one share drops after the split. If a company splits their shares, the number of outstanding shares increase by a specific multiple. The total dollar value of the shares remains the same compared to pre-split amounts, because the split does not add any real value. The most common split ratios are 2-for-1 or 3-for-1, which means that the stockholder will have two or three shares, respectively, for every share held before the split.

In theory, a stock split should have no effect on a stock's price, but it often results in renewed investor interest, which can have a positive impact on the stock price. If the company continues to do well, the dividend may increase at an accelerated rate, and every dividend hike will increase your income on all the shares you own of that stock.

Stock splits may have no effect on the value of the stock, but they do indicate that the company has a history of growth. If a company has split its stock two times in the past twenty years, then the price of the stock (and the dividend) must have doubled at each split. So, I think stock splits do make a difference, proving you have invested in a quality dividend growth stock.

For those who read my first book, *Your Ever Growing Income*, you might recall the foreword by Tom Connolly. He spoke of his purchase of 200 shares of Bank of Nova Scotia (BNS) in 1990, which paid a dividend of 0.25 cents per share. After 28 years and four stock splits, his original cost worked out to $3.64 per share. In 2019, they began receiving $3.60 in dividends per share, or 98.9% of their original investment each year.

Does Income Investing work?

This would seem to be the "million-dollar question", wouldn't it? I have based my first two books on my commitment to this investing philosophy. I have researched, studied, and lived this form of investing for many years, and found great and continued success. But I also want to back up what I believe, not just share it, short of posting my broker statement. So, I feel that this question needs to be answered in a number of ways. It makes sense to expand it into multiple questions:

1. Will your income grow continuously?
2. Will your income grow even if you stop adding funds?
3. Will your income grow even if you pay a high price?
4. Will your income grow if the company(s) do not raise their dividend?

With Income investing, the answer is yes to all four questions, provided:

1. You own quality dividend growth stocks.
2. You reinvest your dividends.
3. The company(s) does not cut their dividend.

I believe these points are best illustrated with an example, and in this case it's a personal one. The following chart shows how my wife invested funds in a bank stock for our grandkids:

	Grandsons Investment				Grand daughters Investment		
Year	Invested amounts	Income Earned	Income Gth % Each Yr.	Year	Invested amounts	Income Earned	Income Gth % Each Yr.
2007	$5,555.00	$0.00		2007	$5,555.00		
2008	$500.00	$217.30		2008	$500.00	$217.30	
2009	$500.00	$253.81	16.80%	2009	$500.00	$253.81	16.80%
2010	$0.00	$281.43	10.88%	2010	$0.00	$281.43	10.88%
2011	$1,000.00	$323.94	15.10%	2011	$1,000.00	$323.94	15.10%
2012	$0.00	$379.31	17.09%	2012	$0.00	$379.31	17.09%
2013	$0.00	$431.66	13.80%	2013	$0.00	$431.66	13.80%
2014	$0.00	$481.32	11.50%	2014	$0.00	$481.32	11.50%
2015	$0.00	$531.84	10.50%	2015	$0.00	$531.84	10.50%
2016	$0.00	$588.67	10.69%	2016	$100.00	$587.10	10.39%
2017	$1,000.00	$655.52	11.36%	2017	$1,200.00	$671.40	14.36%
2018	$0.00	$767.36	17.06%	2018	$2,200.00	$833.38	24.13%
2019	$1,000.00	$893.39	16.42%	2019	$2,200.00	$1,030.90	23.70%

If you review the investment dates and amounts, you will see that:

- The larger initial funds were invested before the financial crisis of late 2008 and 2009, meaning she paid a high price for the shares.
- Money was not added to buy more shares every year.

INCOME INVESTING EXPLAINED

- The income earned shows a steadily increasing income from the investment, each and every year.
- The income growth percentage averaged 13.72% from 2009 thru 2019 for our grandson and 15.75% for our granddaughter.
- Not mentioned or shown on the chart is that this bank stock did not increase their dividend for 2 1/2 years.

You might wonder why our granddaughter generated a much higher income growth for the last three years. She took over her DRIP account when she turned 18, and began adding $100 per month to the account. Those additional contributions resulted in a higher income and the higher income growth rate each year. That's the power of compounding.

I think this example does a good job illustrating how Income investing works, and works well.

I am also happy to show you another example as further proof. This is from my second book, *The TFSA Compounder*. It shows how I have contributed the maximum allowed to my TFSA account since its inception in 2009, right up to 2019. I have only invested in dividend growth stocks, not bought and sold stocks, and currently own only four company stocks from the TSX 60. The following chart shows my TFSA contributions each year and the dividend income Ihave received. For comparison, the right side of the chart shows what would have happened if I had invested the same amounts, during the same

Hm TFSA	Invested Amount	Dividend Income	XIU ETF	Invested Amount	Distribution Income
2009	5,000	144.94	2009	5,000	173.88
2010	5,000	399.00	2010	5,000	288.94
2011	5,000	862.35	2011	5,000	410.87
2012	5,000	959.70	2012	5,000	589.00
2013	5,500	1,313.46	2013	5,500	857.74
2014	5,500	1,742.35	2014	5,500	957.39
2015	10,000	2,404.75	2015	10,000	1395.78
2016	5,500	3,301.78	2016	5,500	1211.18
2017	5,500	3,813.66	2017	5,500	1881.72
2018	5,500	4,574.95	2018	5,500	2243.29
2019	6,000	5,432.10	2019	6,000	2656.81

periods, in the XIU ETF (which emulates the TSX 60 Index):

As of 2019, my TFSA is providing 105% more income than I would have earned if the funds had been invested in the XIU ETF, over the 11-year period.

My TFSA holds just four dividend growth stocks from the TSX 60, not all sixty that XIU does. Owning all the stocks of an Index dilutes your income as this comparison demonstrates.

I always find it remarkable that so many advisors push Index funds. It has not taken much research, and a fairly simple calculation, to prove the average performance of this particular ETF, especially when comparing it to the success of Income investing. Yet, ETFs continue to grow in popularity (though I feel their popularity does not grow as fast as my income!)

I hope that if you are new to this investment strategy, or curious about how it works, I have shown you that it does indeed work. You don't need any special skills or knowledge, you don't need to be constantly seeking new potential winning stocks, you don't need to be looking for the best time to buy or sell your stocks, you don't need to be widely diversified or re-balance your holdings; Simply identify a few good stocks, buy them at a reasonable price and reinvest the dividends. Continue to add to the stocks you already own or add other quality stocks, as you wish. And of course, enjoy monitoring your progress and watching your income grow!

What is a reasonable Income return?

If we were investing for capital appreciation, we'd expect to at least receive market returns, but because I'm referring to investing for Income, we invest differently from most. Therefore, we should then expect our returns to be different, shouldn't we?

I measure my returns by the percentage growth of the income from my entire portfolio. Some stocks do better than others, some increase their dividend more than others and some just grow at a steady but continuous rate. But overall, I expect my total income to grow by a minimum of 7% to 10% each year. I actually expect that most quality dividend growth portfolios will produce higher income growth percentage each year, but as with any form of investing, you cannot predict nor guarantee any returns. But the proof is in the pudding, I have been investing with this strategy long enough and have seen the success first hand.

Your returns will vary depending upon a number of factors, many beyond your control and the control of the individual companies you will invest in.

But by following the Income Growth Investment Strategy, you should expect to see your income grow slowly and steadily each and every year. We also want our **yield on total investment** to grow, providing us with more income, and generating more income with less money invested than you'd expect. And yes, you will see your capital appreciate, likely very close to your income growth rate. Benefit upon benefit. I find this very "reasonable", don't you?

Should you increase your fixed assets as you age?

Most advisors and most investors believe you should maintain a portion of your investments in fixed assets. The amount one should hold varies, but generally, it is recommended that you increase your fixed assets as you age:

> *"In age-based asset allocation, the investment decision is based on the age of the investors. Therefore, most financial advisors advise investors to make the stock investment decision based on a deduction of their age from a base value of a 100. The figure depends on the life expectancy of the investor. The higher the life expectancy, the higher the portion. That's why the base value may change to 110, or 120".*

The chart below shows the common recommendation of fixed assets one should hold according to their age:

Age	Fixed Asset Allocation
35	20% to 25%
45	30% to 35%
55	40% to 45%
65	55% to 80%

I don't object to fixed assets, but only for your savings and emergency funds. How much you put aside will depend upon your expense needs, possible health issues, and the security of your income sources. For your investment accounts I suggest you hold 100% in dividend growth equity stocks.

To help you see my point more clearly, below I have provided a comparison to show how one might have done over the past 10 years using a fixed asset investment and five dividend growth stocks. For the fixed assets I selected the highest interest rates available for each year and reinvested the interest at the end of each year. The stock dividends were also reinvested:

Interest rates each year:

2009	2.65%
2010	3.83%
2011	3.35%
2012	1.93%
2013	1.85%
2014	2.75%
2015	1.68%
2016	2.03%
2017	2.48%
2018	2.47%
2019	2.79%

Fixed asset investment of $10,000 comparison to five dividend growth stocks, showing market value:

	$10,000 Invested, Income Re-invested					
	GIC/Bonds	Stock #1	Stock #2	Stock #3	Stocks #4	Stocks #5
2009	$10,000	$10,000	$10,000	$10,000	$10,000	$10,000
2010	$10,265	$12,223	$11,279	$11,977	$11,023	$14,343
2011	$10,658	$15,552	$12,116	$12,589	$11,912	$18,176
2012	$11,015	$16,377	$12,033	$12,973	$13,687	$21,499
2013	$11,228	$18,886	$14,757	$14,847	$17,644	$26,492
2014	$11,436	$24,541	$18,752	$19,610	$21,186	$28,891
2015	$11,750	$23,595	$19,844	$18,729	$17,881	$34,022
2016	$11,947	$27,140	$22,424	$18,541	$20,874	$34,525
2017	$12,190	$28,180	$25,924	$23,033	$28,375	$39,535
2018	$12,492	$28,586	$26,336	$24,986	$32,898	$39,730
2019	$12,801	$35,097	$19,234	$24,437	$33,835	$42,007
Income 2019	$199	$1,607	$993	$1,162	$1,214	$1,835

As you can see, Stock #2 had the poorest price growth of the five stocks, but even then, the capital appreciation was 53% higher than the fixed asset after 10 years. Stock #2 also provided the lowest income after 10 years (last line on the chart), but the income is still 400% above the fixed asset in 2019.

I didn't even allow for the 2020 Covid-19 crisis, did I? Well, taking the global health crisis into account, the markets dropped 35% at the lowest point, but recovered enough so that it's only down about 15%, as of this writing. But even with a 35% drop, Stock#2 would be valued about the same as the fixed asset, and with the recovery it would be worth 27.7% more than the fixed asset. The income from Stock #2 has not dropped and will have increased during

2020. I hope it is plain to see that fixed assets, as an investment, just doesn't cut the mustard.

If you want to keep a portion of your funds in fixed assets, you might be protecting your capital, but at what cost? I have shown that you not only risk losing the capital growth that quality stocks offer, but also that the income fixed assets provide simply cannot match the income from quality dividend growth stocks. The interest earned from fixed assets will barely keep up with inflation and your capital will likely lose value because of its lower purchasing power. It is clear that fixed asset investments are a lose-lose scenario to me.

Should you invest in gold?

There is something inherently comforting when it comes to gold, as a personal item and an investment asset. Some of the reasons people have invested specifically in gold are the following:

1. Owning gold can act as a hedge against inflation and deflation alike, it is also considered a good portfolio diversifier.
2. Gold can provide financial security during geopolitical and macroeconomic uncertainty.
3. Gold is a liquid asset, which can be easily turned into cash.

The above chart might be impressive and even have an investor believing that gold should be a good investment. But to me, gold is an asset that only a pessimist might invest in. I think that you buy gold because you believe bad things will happen, for when they do, gold rises in value. The problem is that the value of gold drops when a crisis has passed, and then so does the value in your gold holdings.

For example, if you bought 35 oz. of gold in 2008, before the financial crisis, at $910 per ounce, you would have been investing $31,850.00 (the circled price on the chart above). A quick glance shows that if you had sold that gold between 2012 and 2013 you would have almost doubled your money. But the value of gold dropped after the recovery and did not rise again until the Covid-19 crisis of 2020. Clearly gold does indeed go up in value when a crisis occurs, but as with any investment, we do not know what the future holds. I don't think it is worth holding gold over the long-term, waiting for some kind of crisis lottery win. Too much time is wasted that is better spent accruing gains from solid investing. The other thing to remember is that those who buy gold would likely never sell when the price of gold is rising. They expect the price to go even higher, just as most speculators do.

To illustrate my point further, let's compare how one might have done if they had invested that same $31,850.00 in two dividend growth stocks. I have picked Fortis (FTS) and

	Gold	% Chg	FTS	% Chg	NA	% Chg
2008	$31,850		$18,350		$13,500	
2009	$28,000	-12.09%	$19,604	6.83%	$18,351	35.93%
2010	$38,500	20.88%	$24,058	31.10%	$20,229	49.84%
2011	$49,000	53.85%	$24,026	30.93%	$21,886	62.12%
2012	$56,000	75.82%	$25,811	40.66%	$25,174	86.48%
2013	$59,500	86.81%	$23,770	29.53%	$31,788	135.47%
2014	$42,000	31.87%	$31,086	69.41%	$39,435	192.11%
2015	$42,000	31.87%	$31,966	74.20%	$33,688	149.54%
2016	$33,250	4.40%	$36,191	97.23%	$39,317	191.24%
2017	$32,550	2.20%	$41,764	127.59%	$53,472	296.09%
2018	$43,750	37.36%	$41,935	128.53%	$64,642	378.83%
2019	$42,700	34.07%	$52,983	188.74%	$63,866	373.08%
			Combined FTS & NA Value		$116,849	266.87%

National Bank (NA) to use in this example.

At the end of 2019, the 35 oz. of gold was worth $42,700.00. However, Fortis was worth $52,653.00 and National $75,878.00, for a total of $116,849.00 at the end of 2019. The stocks are worth 173.65% more than the gold! Although gold has risen in value due to the 2020 Covid-19 crisis, and stocks have dropped slightly, they will still out-perform the value of gold, especially over the long-term.

The previous chart shows the market value of gold compared to Fortis and National bank, but remember I always say to invest to generate Income, and ignore capital appreciation altogether. Below is the income comparison of investing the same amount in gold or Fortis and National bank, over the

Investment	Gold $31,850	Income Earned FTS $18,350	NA $13,500
2008	$0	$509.30	$171.45
2009	$0	$636.94	$713.86
2010	$0	$712.11	$746.69
2011	$0	$786.24	$857.72
2012	$0	$850.76	$1,314.99
2013	$0	$935.21	$1,154.33
2014	$0	$1,012.54	$1,326.08
2015	$0	$1,107.46	$1,473.27
2016	$0	$1,293.89	$1,687.15
2017	$0	$1,420.81	$1,879.62
2018	$0	$1,566.08	$2,091.95
2019	$0	$1,721.62	$2,369.31
Total	0	$12,552.94	$15,786.42
		Total FTS & NA	$28,339.37

same period of time:

You can see that over this twelve-year period, an investment in the two dividend growth stocks would have generated $28,339.00 in dividends, almost equal to the total initial investment of $31,850.00 in gold, which generated zero income. And that does not even include the difference in the capital value of the stocks over gold, regardless of which date is chosen.

Gold may be a hedge against inflation and possibly a cushion against economic crisis, but is it really better than investing your money in quality dividend growth stocks? I hope I have proven it's not the treasure at the end of the rainbow that most people believe it is!

Chapter 5

Is it ever too late to start investing for Income?

The simple answer is No. But I do want to stress that the income you can expect to earn or generate will be dependent upon your financial situation. I also want to be honest, as well, and mention that if you are in your 50s or 60s and have not yet saved sufficient money for retirement, then it is unlikely you'll be able to generate enough income to live off ONLY the income from your investments. Investing for income does require a certain amount of time in, to do what it does best.

Furthermore, if you are over 50 and still carrying significant debt, then I feel that debt reduction should be your first priority. But if your debt is manageable, and you have current investments and more funds to invest, then I'd seriously consider switching to investing for Income.

I've heard people say again and again "I just can't save enough to make a difference". I understand that many people live paycheque to paycheque, even as they approach retirement age. But I offer that if they could buckle down, and find a way to save even $1,500.00 a year, and begin investing for Income for the next 10 years, they could easily earn an extra $90.00 a month, or about $1,800.00 a year of extra income. If you continue saving $1,500.00 per year, for another 5 years, then that monthly income increases to $190.00 a month or $2,280.00 a year. Even better, if you invested that $1,500.00 per year into a TFSA, that monthly income will be tax-free, making the purchasing power of the income much higher. One of the best reasons to invest for Income is that it is a continual money generator. Even if you need to withdraw funds (tax-free), any monies left in the account will continue to grow. If possible, I'd suggest that you leave the initial investment in the account and only withdraw the dividends (income). This way you will always have a continual source of income, a living wage, so to speak.

In my opinion, there is NO VALID REASON not to save, at any age. I'd like you to think of it this way, wouldn't any amount of supplemental income that helps to offset monthly expenses during your retirement, when people often have no other way of earning income, be welcome? Especially if you don't have a company pension and must rely just on CPP and OAS. It is a known, and uncomfortable fact, that most people working in the private sector are not covered by company pensions. And government benefits are not growing sufficiently enough to offset inflation.

*I recommend reading "How to Retire the Cheapskate Way" by Jeff Yeager. It's loaded with easy, common-sense ways to reduce your expenses, provides great saving tips and ways to get a *"return on **non-investment**" (as in "NOT SPENDING!")*

Income investing works at any age and at any income level, because, as the name suggests, it's about earning Income from your investments, not about "growing the pile" or watching market prices. When you add time in, not just more money, I believe that everyone can benefit from generating an income from their investments, especially if they have the discipline to not touch their investments until retirement. So, people who often think they have aged out of saving for retirement but expect to keep working and earning for some time yet, will still be able to supplement their government benefits by investing for Income.

I have found that, generally, older investors have accumulated larger amounts of savings or investments. But this is no reason to be complacent about their investments. If they are ready and willing, they will be in a good position to generate higher income immediately. Even better, if you are one of the fortunate, and have managed to become debt-free and have considerable savings, you will have more than sufficient opportunity to achieve the desired goal of living off the income from your investments alone.

Because capital preservation is always a concern for older investors, I strongly recommend that all stock investments be made in the highest quality dividend growth stocks you can find. Don't speculate or seek higher yielding stocks. Stick with the best of the best and take comfort in knowing that your investments will be as safe and more productive than any fixed asset product. The sectors I suggest that would offer the best choices of quality stocks are utilities, banks, communications, railway and possibly a food retailer.

Keep in mind the tax consequences for all of your investments, so choose the stocks which will offer the safest dividend growth with the least amount of tax. The next section will be dealing with withdrawal plans for your investments.

Through my own personal experience, I would like to recommend to anyone 60 years and older to try to maintain a cash reserve for emergency or unforeseen expenses (actually, everyone at any age would be well to do this). Each person should assess their own needs, determine an appropriate amount and keep it separate from their investments. I also think it is very important to keep in mind that people are living longer than ever, especially if you are in good health. The last thing you want is to do is outlive your savings. I have found that investing for Income provides a very important advantage with its continual source of funds, offsetting this potential financial disaster.

If you are fortunate enough to have a secure company pension and believe that the majority of your retirement expenses will be comfortably met, Income growth investment should still be considered. Even if you may not need the money, why not grow your estate for your dependents or donate to charities? Having such choices is a very ideal retirement indeed.

Do you have a withdrawal plan for the future?

In my second book, *The TFSA Compounder*, I suggested, upon retirement, that one draw from their RRSP and company pensions first. I would like to elaborate on this with an actual withdrawal plan. If you have not yet reached retirement, it is a good idea to evaluate your own situation in advance and ask yourself the following questions:

At what age are you planning to retire?

What sources of income will be available?

How much do you think you will need to meet your expenses?

There is no one strategy to suit every person and situation when it comes to a retirement withdrawal plan, so I suggest you consider the tax consequences to help with this decision.

Tax consequences:

- Any **"earned"** income must be included as taxable income at your combined marginal tax rate (the tax rate paid on the next dollar of income, the higher the income the higher the taxes).
- Interest income is taxed at your combined marginal tax rate. If you hold any GICs, Bonds or Bond ETFs, you must pay tax every year on the interest income received, whether you buy the bond at face value, at a discount, or at a premium.
- Taxpayers who hold Canadian dividend-paying stocks in a taxable account are eligible for the dividend tax credit. This means that dividend income will be taxed at a lower rate than the same amount of interest income. Investors in the highest tax bracket pay tax of 29% on dividends, compared to about 50% on interest income.
- Withdrawal from an RRSP must be included as income and is subject to income tax at your combined marginal tax rate.
- At age 71 your RRSP must be converted to a RRIF account. One is required to withdraw a prescribed annual percentage each year, which is subject to income tax at your combined marginal tax rate.
- Canada Pension, Old Age Security and company pensions are taxed as earned income and is subject to income tax at your combined marginal tax rate.

Note: Canada Pension Plan (CPP) benefits can be drawn as early as age 60, but the payment amount is reduced by 0.6% for each month before 65. The reason to consider drawing CPP early is if you need the money, or perhaps you are dealing with a life expectancy that may be reduced due to health issues. Delaying CPP at age 65 increases the amount it will eventually pay by 0.7% for each month until age 70.

If you delay receiving your Old Age Security (OAS) pension at age 65, your monthly pension payment will be increased by 0.6% for every month you delay, from age 65 up to a maximum of 36% at age 70.

- In Canada, 50% of the value of any capital gains (such as the sale of stocks) are taxable. Should you sell the investments at a higher price than you paid (realized capital gain) — you'll need to add 50% of the capital gain to your income. Investors in the highest tax bracket pay tax of 25% on capital gains. When you have an allowable capital loss, perhaps from the sale of investments in a non-registered account, in the current tax year, you can claim it to offset any capital gains. You can only use capital losses to reduce capital gains.

Withdrawals:

Regardless of what age you are able to retire, I suggest taking funds from your TFSAs **as the last resort**. Leave them be, they will continue to compound and grow your tax-free income as long as you let them. Continue contributing the maximum annual amounts to your TFSA, even if the funds, or shares, are transferred from your RRSP, RRIF, or non-registered accounts.

Draw from your taxable sources first; RRSP, company pension, CPP/OAS and possibly dividends from a non-registered account. If you are uncertain about which will result in the least tax, I suggest consulting your accountant.

I have received questions about how one withdraws their dividends, so I'll expand on that here:

- Dividends within an RRSP or RRIF are just part of the income or value of the account and any withdrawals will be considered taxable income.

- Dividends from a non-registered account are taxed in the year they are earned, regardless if you reinvest them or not. If you allow the dividends to accumulate, rather than reinvesting them, you can transfer them periodically to your bank account. Depending upon the broker, there may be a fee to transfer funds to your bank account.
- Another option is to transfer non-registered qualifying company shares to a company Dividend Reinvestment Plan (DRIP). Qualifying companies will be registered with a DRIP Agent, likely Computershare or AST Canada. Once the shares have been transferred, you can instruct the Agent to have the dividend deposited directly into your bank when paid by the company. No fees or hassle.

How do I get kids interested?

Parental harping about saving for the future or trying to teach kids how to spend money more wisely does not really work. But don't let that stop you from talking to them about financial matters, keep trying to teach them the value of money and make them aware of how much things cost. Often these conversations can start when you open their first savings account. For older children, introducing them to the TFSA is a great way to both emphasize saving and teach them about the income tax system.

I think getting kids to recognize the advantages of saving and the potential wealth that investments can provide, is a long-term process that requires a maturing mindset. Still, I believe there are a couple of ways to get them to see the benefit of having investments, even while still quite young:

1. Don't try to teach them about investing until they are old enough to understand, but make them aware of it, perhaps by sharing your own experiences with them.
2. If you start an RESP account, review the results with them on a quarterly basis or at least annually. Show them how much the funds are growing and earning. Hopefully they will see continuous growth

from their portfolio and get excited about that growth.

3. If you are able to open an investment account for them when they are very young, it's okay to remind them that it is their money and periodically show them how much they are earning.
4. If you have invested for Income, write down on the calendar or kitchen note board how much income your portfolio is earning for you each month. You could even have them write down the amount so they can see that it's continually growing.
5. Discuss your own history of investing when you were younger. Talk about how much you tried to save when you were their age. Even better is if you can show them how you tried to increase your savings as you earned more, especially if it's through the Income strategy!
6. If you are planning large purchases, like a car, new appliances, or even electronics that your kids will get particular pleasure out of, get them involved so they understand how much the items cost and how they will be paid for. Take the opportunity to discuss why it's best not to borrow money to pay for these items, or how important it is to save up for these kinds of purchases.
7. Talk about your investment goals and how your investment income is growing slowly and steadily. If you feel investing for the future is important, explain it to them, and hopefully they'll learn the lesson as well.
8. Encourage your kids to begin earning their own money as soon as possible. Suggest baby-sitting, delivering papers, cutting grass, snow shoveling, and part-time work when they are old enough. They don't need to invest any of the money, but the sooner they understand how hard it is to earn money, the better.
9. Talk to them about debt, borrowing, the high cost of credit card charges, and how long it would take to pay back large debts, like student loans.
10. Talk about the advantages of opening a TFSA account, and contributing to one as soon as they begin working full time.
11. Try to avoid discussing the lure of the stock market, and get-rich-quick schemes. Income investors do not watch the stock market, nor get emotional over highs and lows. If anything, emphasize your lack

of interest in the stock market and the price of the shares you own. Later when they understand Income investing you can show them how the capital has also grown.

The main point I want to make is that investing is not just an adult activity. In fact, the sooner a person gets started, and I mean in their youth, the better off they will be when it really matters. I know it is hard to get young people to think about their retirement, but Income investing is about celebrating slow and steady growth. And who else is better suited to a long investing experience than our young people. You may have to do all the work initially, but as they keep seeing their income from the investments grow, without any effort on their part, they will begin to recognize what's happening. The money you invested for them is growing all on its own.

And with Income investing you are not depending on speculation or changing market returns. You get real income deposited steadily and regularly, that grows over time. That's a simple concept for young people to grasp, "money coming in", and hopefully not only will they get hooked on saving, they'll start to look forward to seeing even more money coming in!

Don't waste your money!

I don't begrudge professional investors/advisors for wanting to be paid for the financial advice they provide. I mean, they do proffer a needed service to people who feel more comfortable leaving investment decisions to others. However, I feel this is a bad idea, and an expensive lesson that one should avoid having to learn.

Investing is often marketed as being overly complicated, even daunting. And if one is investing for capital appreciation, it can be difficult to keep on top of everything that one needs to know to be successful at it.

However, if you are interested in the Income Growth Investment Strategy, learning the process, committed to the implementation of the strategy and continued data tracking, I think you will find it is not that difficult. I can attest to that. I had no training, no experience with investing when I started. I had the same needs and wants of people worried about their retirement and financial security. But I do not trust easily, and when I experienced loss and low returns, I started to look for my own answers and solutions. In the end, I discovered that I was better off making my own decisions and saving money at the same time.

There is next to no need, that I can see, to use pay-for-financial-advice when it comes to identifying dividend growth stocks. There are newsletters, courses and even updates of dividend growth stock lists which are available for a fee, such as those shown below:

INCOME INVESTING EXPLAINED

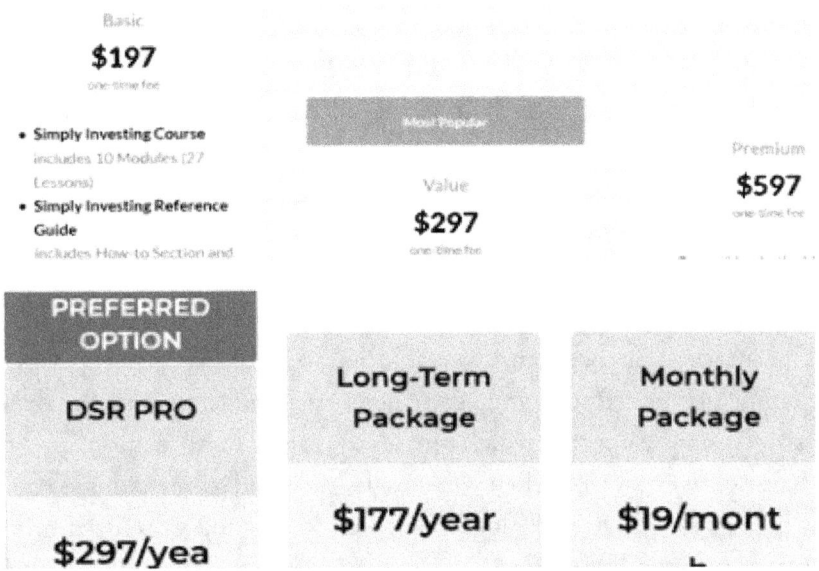

If you are paying for advice, especially if it's an ongoing fee, financial advisors will try to impress you with extensive data and convoluted terms, which I find distracting and unnecessary. I've found that keeping things simple is often the best course of action. Charts and projections are meant to get you excited and optimistic about the future, but too often they are based on past performance and future projections which cannot be confirmed. If you really look into what most advisors offer, you'll see it is often their best guess as to what the market or specific stocks will do in the future. In fact, the majority of professional advisors are focused on price growth and beating the market. That's not what an Income investor should be concerned with and their best guess is as good as yours.

I am a naturally curious person, always taking the opportunity to learn as much as I can about things that interest me. Investing was something that seemed difficult, others appeared to know much more than the average investor, and I believed that financial advisors were people whose advice should be listened to.

I had to learn the hard way that that is not always true. And it is a lesson that I do not want to be taught again. Having money for your retirement is essential, and not something to be taken lightly. With that being said, I find it very strange that so many people are willing to hand over their financial lives without really knowing what is happening. I hope that my books provide an alternative that is accessible and approachable. This latest book is also a continuation of what I have enjoyed doing; learning about investing, making the best decisions for me, and sharing what I have learned along the way.

I want to show that Income investing does not have to be complicated, that almost anyone can grasp the basics of selecting and evaluating stocks, and that the decisions needed to be successful need not be difficult. I want you to learn to take control of your own investments, do your own analysis, make your own decisions, and not assume that others can do a better job than you.

The internet has been an invaluable source and tool in researching and developing my investment strategy. There are a large number of dividend growth sites on the internet which provide a wealth of information, all for free. I do have to mention that when you google "dividend growth blogs" you'll see many listings for "Dividend Blogs". There are some good sites listed, with just as many not-so-good ones too.

I started my own blog, https://risingyieldoninvestments.blogspot.com, after writing my first book, but unfortunately it hasn't made it on to anyone's best-of list yet. Oh well! Funnily enough, neither has Tom Connolly's, who has the best of all sites about dividend growth investing, in my opinion, **http://www.dividendgrowth.ca/dividendgrowth/** or Mark Seed's blog, "MyOwnAdvisor", **https://www.myownadvisor.ca/**, which I believe is also one of the better sites.

I guess what I am trying to say is that I hope you will begin to do your own research and investigations upon learning more about Income investing. There is no shortage of relevant information. And you will come to recognize what is quality over quantity, especially when it comes to choosing dividend growth stocks. I hope that I have set you on a path to independence, both financially and even emotionally. We live in uncertain times, most of us have experienced quite a few ups and downs, and we are all looking for more stability and security in our lives. And I believe financial stability is very attainable and within our reach. You have to believe in yourself, and trust that you have the means, skills and the opportunity to take control of your own financial future.

Accessing the 45 Canadian Stocks

In Chapter 2, I referred to 45 Canadian dividend growth stocks that I suggest you begin your evaluation with. When I compiled the list of the 45 stocks all had raised their dividend for at least eight consecutive years as of 2019. I've listed and grouped them into their 10 market sectors in the chart below:

Symbol	Canadian Company Name	Sector
1 CTC-A	Canadian Tire Corp Ltd A	Consumer Disc
2 DOL	Dollarama Inc.	Consumer Disc
3 EMP-A	Empire Company Ltd	Consumer Disc
4 MRU	Metro Inc	Consumer Disc
5 PLZ-UN	Plaza Retail REIT	Consumer Disc
6 TRI	Thomson Reuters	Consumer Disc

Symbol	Canadian Company Name	Sector
7 ADW-A	Andrew Peller Ltd.	Consumer Stap
8 ATD.B	Alimentation Couche-Tard Inc.	Consumer Stap
9 SAP	Saputo Inc.	Consumer Stap

Symbol	Canadian Company Name	Sector
1 CNQ	Canadian Natural Resources	Energy
2 ENB	Enbridge Inc	Energy
3 IMO	Imperial Oil	Energy
4 TRP	T C Energy	Energy

	Symbol	Canadian Company Name	Sector
1	BAM-A	Brookfield Asset Management Inc	Financials
2	BMO	Bank of Montreal	Financials
3	BNS	Bank of Nova Scotia	Financials
4	CM	Canadian Imperial Bank of Commerce	Financials
5	CWB	Canadian Western Bank	Financials
6	LB	Laurentian Bank Of Canada	Financials
7	MIC	Genworth MI Canada Inc	Financials
8	NA	National Bank	Financials
9	RY	Royal Bank of Canada	Financials
10	TD	Toronto Dominion Bank	Financials

	Symbol	Canadian Company Name	Sector
1	BIP-UN	Brookfield Infrastructure Partners LP	Industrials
2	CAE	CAE Inc	Industrials
3	CNR	Canadian National Railway	Industrials
4	FTT	Finning International	Industrials
5	RBA	Ritchie Bros. Auctioneers Inc	Industrials
6	SJ	Stella-Jones Inc.	Industrials
7	TCL-A	Transcontinental Inc	Industrials
8	TIH	Toromont Industries Ltd	Industrials
9	XTC	Exco Technologies Ltd	Industrials

	Symbol	Canadian Company Name	Sector
1	IFC	Intact Financial	Insurance

	Symbol	Canadian Company Name	Sector
1	CCL-B	CCL Industries Inc	Materials
2	FNV	Franco-Nevada Corp	Materials

	Symbol	Canadian Company Name	Sector
1	ENGH	Enghouse Systems Limited	Technology
1	TCS	Tecsys Inc.	Technology

	Symbol	Canadian Company Name	Sector

	Symbol	Canadian Company Name	Sector
2	BCE	BCE Inc	Telecom
1	CCA	Cogeco Communications Inc	Telecom
1	CGO	Cogeco Inc	Telecom
3	T	Telus Corporation	Telecom
	Symbol	Canadian Company Name	Sector
1	ACO-X	Atco Ltd., Cl.I,	Utilities
2	CU	Canadian Utilities	Utilities
3	EMA	Emera Incorporated	Utilities
4	FTS	Fortis Inc	Utilities

As of this writing only one of the 45 Canadian stocks have cut their dividend during the Covid-19 crisis, and 30, or 67%, have raised their dividend in 2020.

Announcement: May 29, 2020

> "***Laurentian Bank*** *slashed its dividend by 40 per cent on Friday, the first such move by a major Canadian lender in almost three decades".*

Laurentian Bank is the seventh largest bank in Canada, and the dividend cut is likely the result of higher provisions for loan losses to brace for the financial impacts of the coronavirus pandemic.

I suggest you begin the development of your "List of Stocks to Consider" by reviewing these 45 stocks, following the evaluation process described in my earlier books.

When I complete an evaluation and develop my own list, I also like to give each stock a rating. As an example of this, I am now going to review the ten financial stocks and suggest how I rated each of them.

1. First thing I did is apply the Five-rule test to determine how each stock has performed over the past 10 years.
2. The following chart shows the stocks listed alphabetically, with their calculated 10-year dividend

Symbol	Company Name	10-Yr Div Gth	10-Yr Ave Yld
BAM-A	Brookfield Asset Management Inc	86.96%	1.33%
BMO	Bank of Montreal	45.00%	4.13%
BNS	Bank of Nova Scotia	78.06%	4.07%
CM	Canadian Imperial Bank of Commerce	60.92%	4.55%
CWB	Canadian Western Bank	145.45%	2.64%
LB	Laurentian Bank Of Canada	81.94%	4.42%
MIC	Genworth MI Canada Inc	75.42%	4.58%
NA	National Bank	114.52%	3.95%
RY	Royal Bank of Canada	103.52%	3.77%
TD	Toronto Dominion Bank	136.98%	3.47%

growth and average yield, as of this writing.

3. I ranked them according to which ones I felt performed the best over the past 10 years, and even taking into account my personal feelings about each company. The questions about these stocks that arose during my analysis are:

Which ones have had the highest 10-year dividend growth?

Which have had the highest year-to-year dividend growth percentage, over the 10 years (which I did not show in this summary)?

Which ones appear to be in the strongest financial position?

Which ones performed well over a much longer time than my 10-year analysis period?

Which ones recovered the quickest from the financial crisis, or whose prices have dropped the least during the latest crisis?

What is my personal preference about the companies and their products/services?

I used a simple ranking system for each:

A – Really Good

B – Very Good

C – Good

D – Dividend growth stocks which I felt did not make the grade, and will not be added to my list.

1. I ranked each stock separately. I did not necessarily have to give any stock an "A", or I might have wished to give all the stocks in a sector "B" or "C". When you do this exercise, be discerning and particular. Keep in mind that you are trying to create a list of the best of the best stocks you can.

Regardless of how many stocks make your initial list, the decision on how to rate them is yours. Not every sector may have an "A", "B" or even a "C" stock. Assign a rating according to how good or secure you believe they are. You will often find, rather strangely, that stocks rated "C" and "D" will seem the most attractive because they will offer a better current yield. But you may find that over the long-term, you might benefit from paying the higher price for an "A" or "B" stock and accept their lower yields.

I ranked the 10 financial stocks as of this writing, as follows:

A	RY
A	TD
B	BNS
B	NA
C	BAM-A
C	CWB
D	BMO
D	CM
D	LB
D	MIC

*The "D" rated stocks are ones I would reject and would not make my final "List of Stocks to Consider" (as of this evaluation).

When you do your own analysis of these 10 financial stocks, you may rate them differently. There is no right or wrong answer, because the status of the stocks may change when you actually do the analysis. The purpose of evaluating stocks is to screen them for quality and decide which stocks you feel most comfortable with at that time.

Those concerned with diversification might wish to select at least one or more stocks from at least five sectors, to include in your "List of Stocks to Consider". You don't need to own stocks from every sector or own that many stocks overall. Keep in mind the tax implications of owning specific stocks in various accounts.

Follow the same process with the 35 US stocks listed in Appendix B later in the book. Remember that I recommend you only add US stocks in an RRSP. As of this writing none of the 35 US stocks have cut their dividend, but a few have not raised them, as expected, in the first two quarters of 2020.

I have not provided my choices for all 45 stocks, but as I've said before, it is because the status of stocks will change over time. I think it is important that you not concentrate so much on someone else's choices because what were good stocks at the time of this writing may not be as good when you are preparing your list. Stocks will move up and down on your own list over time, some stocks may even get removed and new ones added. I will always encourage investors to educate themselves and stay educated. I don't think anyone can become a financial genius by reading a couple of books (mine included). Good investing, making good choices, is an on-going process that requires diligence and patience. Just as there is no one best list of stocks, my preferences will not always match yours. But I do want the readers of my books to feel that making solid decisions in such unpredictable territory is possible and achievable.

Financial success is a long-haul venture, in my opinion. Likely the stocks which make your "List of Stocks to Consider" will remain on the list for many years, likely 10 years and more.

You do not need to find the best stocks, buy at the best price, or hold the most winners all the time. Not all of your holdings will perform at the same level nor hold that level, but as long as they continue to grow your income, you can and will do well with your investments.

Want to know what would make me the happiest? It would be to know that if you implemented the Income Growth Investment Strategy, followed it for 10 years or more, and at the end of that time you look back on your investments and say: "I'm glad I found Income Investing and it has been the safest and soundest investment I ever made".

Some final comments

1. Investing decisions cannot be clearly defined, because market conditions and changes in the economy will always affect or offer different choices.
2. Yield should be your number one criterion; whether you are considering to buy, sell or measure how well your investment has performed.
3. Diversify, but diversify by selecting amongst the best dividend growth stocks within various sectors.
4. Make your stock choices from just the 1% of the best Canadian & US dividend growth stocks.
5. The basic guidelines presented here, and my other books, may be sufficient to allow you to make investment decisions, but the choice to expand your evaluation criteria and learn other methods to compare your findings as you gain experience, is yours.
6. Don't chase yield. If you have a choice between a stock which offers a reasonable yield and reasonable dividend growth over one which offers a higher yield and a lower growth rate, select the first.
7. If you own lower quality or higher yielding stocks, monitor their progress and look to sell during booming markets. Don't hold off just because you might take a capital loss, consider what might happen if the company cuts their dividend or the market crashes.
8. Look to sell stocks which are not performing as expected when markets are rising.
9. If the market crashes and a company cuts their dividend, that may be the worst time to consider selling. Rather, you may wish to consider the investment a loss leader and hold the stock until the market recovers.
10. During market crashes, look to buy stocks which were previously considered too expensive. Other good stocks may offer better yields,

but this may be the opportunity to own some of the very best stocks at a reasonable price.

Dividend stocks from around the world

I am not sure if readers of this book will be interested in dividend-paying companies from other countries, but there is a website which lists many dividend-paying companies from almost any country. The website is called "Dividend Ranking:"

DIVIDENDS RANKING

http://www.dividendsranking.com/

WARNING: The companies are listed by "highest yield" and I want to stress that no one should assume that stocks offering the highest yield be considered good dividend growth stocks. If anything, any stock with an initial yield above 7% should be viewed with suspect and likely the dividend has a high possibility of being cut.

Country ▼   Industry ▼   Index ▼   Sector

To obtain the list of dividend-paying stocks for a country, simply click on arrow by Country, then click on the country

Full Canada Dividend stocks list

Company	Dividend	Payout	Sector
Husky Energy	11.19%	-35.71%	Oil and Gas Producers
Riocan REIT	9.06%	58.78%	Real Estate Investment Trusts
Power Corp Canada	8.04%	78.17%	Life Insurance
Pembina Pipeline	7.89%	98.05%	Gas Water and Multiutilities
Great-West Lifeco	7.64%	62.50%	Life Insurance
IGM Financial	7.63%	69.44%	Financial Services
Suncor Energy	7.49%	98.94%	Oil and Gas Producers
Canadian Natural Rs	7.29%	37.20%	Oil and Gas Producers
Enbridge	7.09%	109.03%	Oil Equipment Services and Distrib

you wish to see the listing for.

Remember, you should apply my five-rule test before considering any stock listed. If you are evaluating any stock from a foreign country, you may need to search for an online data source, as the ones listed in my books may not provide the dividend data to do your analysis for foreign stocks.

Worksheet to track Monthly Income

I have added a new Excel worksheet to the "Sample Report Cdn New" file, called "Mo Inc". The purpose of this worksheet is to record the monthly dividends received, and your accumulated dividends for the year.

Monthly Dividend Income

	Income by Month	Monthly Increase	Annual Increase	Annual % Growth
Dec-18	$34,597.15			
Jan-19	$35,776.73	$1,179.58	$1,179.58	3.41%
Feb-19	$35,868.09	$91.36	$1,270.94	3.67%
Mar-19	$35,957.84	$89.75	$1,360.69	3.93%
Apr-19	$36,052.06	$94.21	$1,454.91	4.21%
May-19	$36,190.62	$138.56	$1,593.47	4.61%
Jun-19	$36,260.30	$69.68	$1,663.15	4.81%
Jul-19	$36,360.84	$100.54	$1,763.69	5.10%
Aug-19	$36,463.95	$103.11	$1,866.80	5.40%
Sep-19	$36,571.40	$107.45	$1,974.25	5.71%
Oct-19	$36,674.28	$102.88	$2,077.13	6.00%
Nov-19	$36,785.18	$110.90	$2,188.03	6.32%
Dec-19	$36,898.99	$113.81	$2,301.84	6.65%
Jan-20	$37,006.70	$107.71	$107.71	0.29%
Feb-20	$37,116.96	$110.26	$217.97	0.59%
Mar-20	$37,226.69	$109.74	$327.70	0.89%
Apr-20	$37,619.03	$392.34	$720.04	1.95%
May-20	$37,731.01	$111.98	$832.02	2.25%
Jun-20	$37,913.25	$182.24	$1,014.26	2.75%
Jul-20	$38,026.14	$112.90	$1,127.16	3.05%
Aug-20	$38,139.04	$112.90	$1,240.06	3.36%
Sep-20	$0.00	-$38,139.04	-$36,898.99	-100.00%
Oct-20	$0.00	$0.00	-$36,898.99	-100.00%
Nov-20	$0.00	$0.00	-$36,898.99	-100.00%

RIF Withdraw | Mo Inc | Summary

The second column, the "Income by Month" shows your yearly dividend income, which is linked to the "Yearly Div" income from the Summary" report (shown below).

SAMPLE INVESTING SUMMARY

Yearly Div	Ave Yield
$38,139.04	5.315%

The third column shows the dividend income monthly, the forth column is the accumulated dividends for the year, the fourth column is the change in the amount of income for the year and the last column is the income percentage change for the year.

Here is the catch: At the end of each month, once you have recorded all the stock transactions you must change the formula in the "Income by Month" cell to a "Only Values", otherwise the income figures for the previous months will always match the current figure, on the "Summary" report. Here's how you do it:

Look at the formula for "Aug-20", shown below:

B	C	D	E	F
Dec-19	$36,898.99	$113.81	$2,301.84	6.65%
Jan-20	$37,006.70	$107.71	$107.71	0.29%
Feb-20	$37,116.96	$110.26	$217.97	0.59%
Mar-20	$37,226.69	$109.74	$327.70	0.89%
Apr-20	$37,619.03	$392.34	$720.04	1.95%
May-20	$37,731.01	$111.98	$832.02	2.25%
Jun-20	$37,913.25	$182.24	$1,014.26	2.75%
Jul-20	$38,026.14	$112.90	$1,127.16	3.05%
Aug-20	$38,139.04	$112.90	$1,240.05	3.36%

To change it to "Only Values":

- Right click the cell and left click "Copy"

Jul-20	$38,026.14	$112.90
Aug-20	$38,139.04	
Sep-20	$0.00	
Oct-20	$0.00	
Nov-20	$0.00	
Dec-20	$0.00	

Then Right click the cell again, arrow to "Paste Options",

- then arrow to "Values" (V) and left click

	fx	38139.04		
B	C	D	E	F
Dec-19	$36,898.99	$113.81	$2,301.84	6.65%
Jan-20	$37,006.70	$107.71	$107.71	0.29%
Feb-20	$37,116.96	$110.26	$217.97	0.59%
Mar-20	$37,226.69	$109.74	$327.70	0.89%
Apr-20	$37,619.03	$392.34	$720.04	1.95%
May-20	$37,731.01	$111.98	$832.02	2.25%
Jun-20	$37,913.25	$182.24	$1,014.26	2.75%
Jul-20	$38,026.14	$112.89	$1,127.15	3.05%
Aug-20	$38,139.04	$112.90	$1,240.05	3.36%

The figure will no longer contain the formula, just the number. You will have to remember to do this at the end of each month.

To get the new worksheet you will need to download the "Sample Report Cdn New". If you have set up your own worksheet you can then copy the "Mo Inc" worksheet into your file and then enter the monthly dividends or change the formula for each cell to get the "Total Income" figure from your "Summary" report.

Appendix A

45 Canadian Dividend Stocks

	Symbol	Canadian Company Name	Sector
1	ADW-A	Andrew Peller Ltd.	Consumer Stap
2	ACO-X	Atco Ltd., Cl.I,	Utilities
3	ATD.B	Alimentation Couche-Tard Inc.	Consumer Stap
4	BAM-A	Brookfield Asset Management Inc	Financials
5	BCE	BCE Inc	Telecom
6	BIP-UN	Brookfield Infrastructure Partners LP	Industrials
7	BMO	Bank of Montreal	Financials
8	BNS	Bank of Nova Scotia	Financials
9	CAE	CAE Inc	Industrials
10	CCA	Cogeco Communications Inc	Telecom
11	CCL-B	CCL Industries Inc	Materials
12	CGO	Cogeco Inc	Telecom
13	CM	Canadian Imperial Bank of Commerce	Financials
14	CNQ	Canadian Natural Resources	Energy
15	CNR	Canadian National Railway	Industrials
16	CTC-A	Canadian Tire Corp Ltd A	Consumer Disc
17	CU	Canadian Utilities	Utilities
18	CWB	Canadian Western Bank	Financials
19	DOL	Dollarama Inc.	Consumer Disc

Symbol	Canadian Company Name	Sector
20 EMA	Emera Incorporated	Utilities
21 EMP-A	Empire Company Ltd	Consumer Disc
22 ENB	Enbridge Inc	Energy
23 ENGH	Enghouse Systems Limited	Software
24 FNV	Franco-Nevada Corp	Materials
25 FTS	Fortis Inc	Utilities
26 FTT	Finning International	Industrials
27 IFC	Intact Financial	Insurance
28 IMO	Imperial Oil	Energy
29 LB	Laurentian Bank Of Canada	Financials
30 MIC	Genworth MI Canada Inc	Financials
31 MRU	Metro Inc	Consumer Disc
32 NA	National Bank	Financials
33 PLZ-UN	Plaza Retail REIT	Consumer Disc
34 RBA	Ritchie Bros. Auctioneers Inc	Industrials
35 RY	Royal Bank of Canada	Financials
36 SAP	Saputo Inc.	Consumer Stap
37 SJ	Stella-Jones Inc.	Industrials
38 T	Telus Corporation	Telecom

Symbol	Canadian Company Name	Sector
39 TCL-A	Transcontinental Inc	Industrials
40 TCS	Tecsys Inc.	Technology
41 TD	Toronto Dominion Bank	Financials
42 TIH	Toromont Industries Ltd	Industrials
43 TRI	Thomson Reuters	Consumer Disc
44 TRP	T C Energy	Energy
45 XTC	Exco Technologies Ltd	Industrials

Appendix B

35 US Dividend Stocks

	Company Symbol	US Company Name	Sector
1	ADM	ARCHER DANIELS MIDLAND CO	Consumer Staples
2	ADP	AUTOMATIC DATA PROCESSING	Information Tech
3	AOS	A. O. SMITH CORP	Industrials
4	APD	AIR PRODUCTS AND CHEMICALS	Materials
5	AT&T	AT&T	Communication
6	ATO	ATMOS ENERGY	Utilities
7	BDX	BECTON DICKINSON AND CO	Health Care
8	BEN	FRANKLIN RESOURCES INC	Financials
9	CAH	CARDINAL HEALTH INC	Health Care
10	CB	CHUBB LIMITED	Financials
11	CL	COLGATE-PALMOLIVE	Consumer Staples
12	CTAS	CINTAS CORP	Industrials
13	DOV	DOVER CORP	Industrials
14	ECL	ECOLAB INC	Materials
15	EMR	EMERSON ELECTRIC	Industrials
16	GD	GENERAL DYNAMICS CORP	Industrials
17	GWW	W W GRAINGER INC	Industrials
18	HRL	HORMEL FOODS CORP	Consumer Staples

INCOME INVESTING EXPLAINED

Company Symbol	US Company Name	Sector
19 ITW	ILLINOIS TOOL WORKS INC	Industrials
20 JNJ	JOHNSON & JOHNSON	Health Care
21 KO	COCA-COLA CO/THE	Consumer Staples
22 LOW	LOWE'S COS INC	Consumer Discret
23 MCD	MCDONALD'S CORP	Consumer Discret
24 MDT	MEDTRONIC INC	Health Care
25 MKC	MCCORMICK & COMPANY	Consumer Staples
26 MMM	3M CO	Industrials
27 O	REALTY INCOME	Real Estate
28 PG	PROCTER & GAMBLE CO	Consumer Staples
29 PNR	PENTAIR PLC	Industrials
30 ROP	ROPER TECHNOLOGIES	Industrials
31 TGT	TARGET CORP	Consumer Discret
32 TROW	T. ROWE PRICE GROUP INC	Financials
33 WBA	WALGREENS BOOTS ALLIANCE	Consumer Staples
34 WMT	WAL-MART STORES INC	Consumer Staples
35 XOM	EXXON	Energy

Appendix C

TSX 60 Canadian Stocks

	Symbol	Company	Sector
1	AEM	Agnico Eagle Mines Limited	Materials
2	ATD.B	Alimentation Couche-Tard Inc.	Consumer Staples
3	ARX	ARC Resources Ltd.	Energy
4	BMO	Bank of Montreal	Financials
5	BNS	Bank of Nova Scotia	Financials
6	ABX	Barrick Gold Corporation	Materials
7	BHC	Bausch Health Companies Inc.	Health Care
8	BCE	BCE Inc.	Telecom
9	BB	BlackBerry Limited	Information Tech
10	BBD.B	Bombardier Inc.	Industrials
11	BAM.A	Brookfield Asset Management Inc.	Financials
12	CCO	Cameco Corporation	Energy
13	CM	Canadian Imperial Bank of Commerce	Financials
14	CNR	Canadian National Railway Company	Industrials
15	CNQ	Canadian Natural Resources Limited	Energy
16	CP	Canadian Pacific Railway Limited	Industrials
17	CTC.A	Canadian Tire Corporation, Limited	Consumer Disc
18	CCL.B	CCL Industries Inc.	Materials
19	CVE	Cenovus Energy Inc.	Energy
20	GIB.A	CGI Group Inc.	Information Tech
21	CSU	Constellation Software Inc.	Information Tech
22	CPG	Crescent Point Energy Corp.	Energy
23	DOL	Dollarama Inc.	Consumer Disc
24	EMA	Emera Incorporated	Utilities
25	ENB	Enbridge Inc.	Energy

Symbol	Company	Sector
26 ECA	Encana Corporation	Energy
27 FM	First Quantum Minerals Ltd.	Materials
28 FTS	Fortis Inc.	Utilities
29 FNV	Franco-Nevada Corporation	Materials
30 WN	George Weston Limited	Consumer Staples
31 GIL	Gildan Activewear Inc.	Consumer Disc
32 G	Goldcorp Inc.	Materials
33 HSE	Husky Energy Inc.	Energy
34 IMO	Imperial Oil Limited	Energy
35 IPL	Inter Pipeline Ltd.	Energy
36 K	Kinross Gold Corporation	Materials
37 L	Loblaw Companies Limited	Consumer Staples
38 MG	Magna International Inc.	Consumer Disc
39 MFC	Manulife Financial Corporation	Financials
40 MRU	Metro Inc.	Consumer Staples
41 NA	National Bank of Canada	Financials
42 NTR	Nutrien Inc.	Materials
43 OTEX	Open Text Corporation	Information Tech
44 PPL	Pembina Pipeline Corporation	Energy
45 POW	Power Corporation of Canada	Financials
46 QSR	Restaurant Brands International Inc	Consumer Disc

	Symbol	Company	Sector
47	RCI.B	Rogers Communications Inc.	Telecom
48	RY	Royal Bank of Canada	Financials
49	SAP	Saputo Inc.	Consumer Staples
50	SJR.B	Shaw Communications Inc.	Telecom
51	SNC	SNC-Lavalin Group Inc.	Industrials
52	SLF	Sun Life Financial Inc.	Financials
53	ATD.B	Alimentation Couche-Tard Inc	Energy
54	TECK.B	Teck Resources Limited	Materials
55	T	Telus Corporation	Telecom
56	TRI	Thomson Reuters Corporation	Consumer Disc
57	TD	Toronto-Dominion Bank	Financials
58	TRP	TransCanada Corporation	Energy
59	WCN	Waste Connections US Inc.	Industrials
60	WPM	Wheaton Precious Metals Corp	Materials

Appendix D

63 US Dividend Aristocrats

	Symbol	Company Name	Sector
1	MMM	3M Company	Industrials
2	ABBV	AbbVie Inc.	Health Care
3	ABT	Abbott Laboratories	Health Care
4	APD	Air Products & Chemicals Inc	Materials
5	ALB	Albemarle Corporation	Materials
6	AMCR	Amcor plc	Materials
7	AOS	A.O. Smith	Industrials
8	ADM	Archer Daniels Midland	Consumer Staples
9	T	AT&T	Communication
10	ATO	Atmos Energy	Utilities
11	ADP	Automatic Data Processing	Information Tech
12	BDX	Becton Dickinson	Health Care
13	BF-B	Brown-Forman Class B	Consumer Staples
14	CAH	Cardinal Health Inc.	Health Care
15	CAT	Caterpillar Inc.	Industrials
16	CVX	Chevron Corp.	Energy
17	CB	Chubb Limited	Financials
18	CINF	Cincinnati Financial Corp	Financials

Symbol	US Company Name	Sector
19 CTAS	Cintas Corp	Industrials
20 CLX	The Clorox Company	Consumer Staples
21 KO	Coca-Cola Co	Consumer Staples
22 CL	Colgate-Palmolive	Consumer Staples
23 ED	Consolidated Edison Inc	Utilities
24 DOV	Dover Corp	Industrials
25 ECL	Ecolab Inc	Materials
26 EMR	Emerson Electric	Industrials
27 ESS	Essex Property Trust	Real Estate
28 EXPD	Expeditors Int. of Washington	Industrials
29 XOM	Exxon Mobil Corp	Energy
30 FRT	Federal Realty Investment Trust	Real Estate
31 BEN	Franklin Resources	Financials
32 GD	General Dynamics	Industrials
33 GPC	Genuine Parts Company	Consumer Discret
34 HRL	Hormel Foods Corp	Consumer Staples
35 ITW	Illinois Tool Works	Industrials
36 JNJ	Johnson & Johnson	Health Care
37 KMB	Kimberly-Clark	Consumer Staples
38 LEG	Leggett & Platt	Consumer Discret
39 LIN	Linde plc	Materials
40 LOW	Lowe's Companies, Inc.	Consumer Discret
36 JNJ	Johnson & Johnson	Health Care
37 KMB	Kimberly-Clark	Consumer Staples
38 LEG	Leggett & Platt	Consumer Discret

Symbol	US Company Name	Sector
39 LIN	Linde plc	Materials
40 LOW	Lowe's Companies, Inc.	Consumer Discret
41 MKC	McCormick & Company	Consumer Staples
42 MCD	McDonald's	Consumer Discret
43 MDT	Medtronic	Health Care
44 NUE	Nucor	Materials
45 PPG	PPG Industries	Materials
46 PEP	PepsiCo	Consumer Staples
47 PNR	Pentair	Industrials
48 PBCT	People's United Financial	Financials
49 PG	Procter & Gamble	Consumer Staples
50 O	Realty Income	Real Estate
51 ROP	Roper Technologies	Industrials
52 ROST	Ross Stores	Consumer Discret
53 SPGI	S&P Global (McGraw Hill, Inc)	Financials
54 SHW	Sherwin-Williams	Materials
55 SWK	Stanley Black & Decker Inc.	Industrials
56 SYY	Sysco	Consumer Staples
57 TROW	T. Rowe Price	Financials
58 TGT	Target Corporation	Consumer Discret
59 UTX	United Technologies Corporation	Industrials
60 VFC	VF Corporation	Consumer Discret
61 GWW	W. W. Grainger	Industrials
62 WMT	Walmart	Consumer Staples
63 WBA	Walgreens Boots Alliance	Consumer Staples

Web Site Resources

Dividend History:
https://dividendhistory.org/

Yahoo Finance:
https://ca.finance.yahoo.com/quote/ENB.TO/history?ltr=1
https://ca.finance.yahoo.com/

Canadian Shareowner Investments Inc.
http://www.investments.shareowner.com/home/v1/index.html

Morningstar home page:
https://www.morningstar.ca/ca/membership/FeatureMatrix.aspx#334-hidenews[1]

The Dividend Channel:
https://www.dividendchannel.com/history/?symbol=xiu.ca

Dividend Growth Investing & Retirement:
https://www.dividendgrowthinvestingandretirement.com/canadian-dividend-all-star-list/

DividendRanking:
http://www.dividendsranking.com/

---

1. https://www.morningstar.ca/ca/membership/FeatureMatrix.aspx%25252523334-hidenews

My Other Books:

Published in 2018, this book introduced the Income Growth Investment Strategy. It provides a detailed evaluation process and an easy-to-follow method for financial success.

This is the US edition, which concentrates on US stocks for those who want to follow the Income Growth Investment Strategy in the American market.

The TFSA Compounder, shows you the advantages of investing in a TFSA first, before any other financial investments. It details how one can obtain financial freedom by combining your TFSA with the Income Growth Investment Strategy.

About the Author

My name is Henry Mah and I'm just an average investor. I learned about the dividend growth strategy from others, followed the strategy for many years, and eventually generated sufficient income from my investments to be able to live off the income, without needing to sell any of the capital.

The books I've written, *Your Ever Growing Income, Your TFSA Compounder* and this current book, were intended to teach those who might be interested in learning how my wife and I achieved financial success by following a dividend growth investment strategy, (what I now call the Income Growth Investment Strategy). I've found this investment strategy simple to learn, easy to implement, one that produces very positive results and does not require one to watch or worry about market fluctuations and stock prices.

The lessons I've learned from others and how I was able to simplify many of the processes should help those willing to follow the Income Growth Investment Strategy to achieve their own goal of generating sufficient investment income to meet their retirement needs.

If you would like to share your views on this book, please add a comment or review on the Amazon website. For those who might have questions, you can email me at:

HMyourgrowingincome@gmail.com

In addition, please visit my blog where I try to post additional articles on the benefits of Income investing:

https://risingyieldoninvestments.blogspot.com/

I wish you well with your investments.